Changing Lakeland

PATTERDALE FARMER

Changing Lakeland

by

W. R. Mitchell

Foreword by

Betty Wainwright

SKIPPER OF THE "TEAL", WINDERMERE

DALESMAN BOOKS
1989

The Dalesman Publishing Company Ltd.,
Clapham, Lancaster, LA2 8EB
First Published 1989
© W.R. Mitchell, 1989

ISBN: 0 85206 971 5

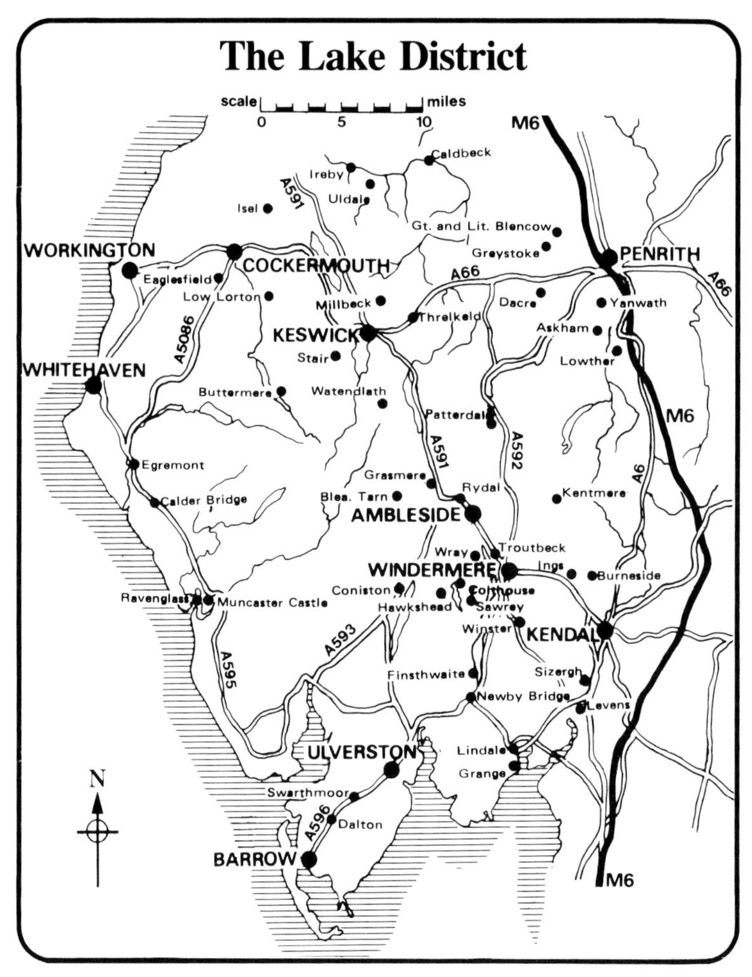

PRINTED BY SMITHS OF BRADFORD

CONTENTS

JOE WELLS, OF MARTINDALE, WITH A HAND-REARED STAG.

PHOTOGRAPHS

(all uncredited photographs by the author)

"RAVEN" AT BOWNESS

INTRODUCTION

IN HIGH PLACES

AFLOAT IN LAKELAND

LIFE IN THE DALES

DANGER: MEN AT WORK

TRAVELLERS ALL

WARTIME INTERLUDE

ONE OR TWO CHARACTERS

CARING FOR LAKELAND

FOREWORD
by Betty Wainwright

BILL MITCHELL'S versatile pen has commented on the Lakeland scene for almost half a century, first as a journalist and then for over 30 years until his retirement in 1988 as Editor of the monthly magazine *Cumbria.*

Retirement, however, has not meant the end of his literary career; rather he has seen it as an opportunity to relate and publish material on various subjects showing his wide diversity of interests: the Settle-Carlisle railway, Elgar and remoter Scotland. Throughout his life he has forged a close affinity with the Yorkshire Dales and Cumbria, meeting the dalesfolk and recording their domestic environment and traditional crafts and activities over the years. His recent book, *The Changing Dales,* illustrated by many photographs of days that are gone, reports the changes that have taken place in the Yorkshire Dales over the past forty years.

Now, in this present volume, he has performed a similar service for the Lake District, his recollections of personal experiences in times past leading to a review of the man-made and accelerating changes that have transformed the valleys and villages of Lakeland in the post-war years, not all of them for the better. Newcomers to the district will be surprised by his account of the Lakeland scene only a short lifetime ago, and old-timers will find pleasure in refreshing their fading memories of the happy days of their youth amongst the fells.

IN THE PICTURE is the kitchen of a fellside farm in 1900. Notice the crane and crook, and the grate beneath, also the "Glendinning" oven. Behind the chair (right) but in shadow is the bake-stone and its fireplace. It was used for making oatcakes, then a prominent feature of the diet. Under the kitchen window stands a bink, or stone table, this one resting on masonry. The floor of this kitchen is flagged.

A popular make of Lakeland fireplace had an oven on one side and a boiler on the other. The kitchen fire was kept roaring the year through, even on hot summer days, to provide a constant source of hot water. At Seathwaite, I was told that the fire was made with some "larch chats", to which kindling sticks were added, followed by coal. The folk at Seathwaite visited Keswick once a month with a horse and cart. Coal was purchased from a dealer at the railway station.

Old-time fireplaces were given liberal coverings of "black lead", applied with a small brush. At a farm in Mardale, it was customary to mix the black lead with some metholated spirits to make it go further! Sweeping the kitchen was done with a besom, made of "birch chat" gathered from the mosses. A besom could get into the cracks and crannies. It was kept dry or it would be attacked by fungus.

Many a farm had a "set pot" for the weekly wash. The farmer's wife would add some soap to the water so that her husband would not be tempted to use it for mixing the calf food!

INTRODUCTION

SOMEWHERE between Hawkshead and Ambleside, I slept in a bed that had a lumpy mattress and a cast iron frame. The householder had achieved the near-impossible feat of setting it up in a bedroom so small that when I was fully stretched I felt the pressure of my head against one wall and the pressure of my feet against another. Forty years ago, bed and breakfast establishments were much less common than they are today. It was also the age before divans, electric blankets, bedside lamps with fancy shades, fitted carpets, a suite with bath and toilet and also facilities for making tea and coffee.

The bedroom was the meeting place of a dozen eager draughts. An all-pervading odour, that of paraffin, would in due course be joined by that of bacon being fried. Every joint of the bed squeaked, so I trained myself to lie still. I awoke as grey light began to seep through windows suffering from condensation and between the thin curtains. Ten minutes went by before I heard a sound. Then, afar off, towards Langdale, a raven uttered its gruff call.

I accepted that the linoleum would be chilly to the bare feet and that survival would depend on getting dressed quickly and dashing downstairs to where a paraffin stove had been placed beside a table in the breakfast room, which in this case was also the parlour. It was the usual splendid Lakeland breakfast, home-cured, farmyard-laid and home-cooked. The charge for bed and breakfast was a few shillings and the housewife gave me some sandwiches and a slab of fruit cake to sustain me during the coming day. I sauntered forth into a Lakeland countryside wearing its Joseph's coat of many colours.

I had just taken over the Editorship of *Cumbria*, a magazine founded by the Lakeland YHA which was offered to the Dalesman Publishing Company in 1951. I ventured into a Lake District that remained in a time-warp; the way of life in the dales between the fell ranges had not greatly changed for many years. Norse terms peppered the dialect and formed the language of topography. Three counties – Cumberland, Westmorland and Lancashire – had wedge-shaped slices of the Lakeland "cake". I did not have to look hard to find local people ("offcomers" formed a small minority of the population) and, when found, most residents would chat entertainingly about t'auld days.

The day that ended with the squeaky bed near Hawkshead had begun with a crossing of Windermere lake on a coal-fired ferryboat. I then walked through the Beatrix Potter countryside, meeting a farmer who was laboriously spreading lime from heaps, using a fork. "I wasn't born here", he said, adding: "But I've bin here a gay lang while". He mentioned days long gone when it was a matter of "blood for money". As a farm lad earning "next to nowt" he had been called to work "from dayleet to dark". In summer, "our shoes were nivver cold".

Change has been in the nature of things since the beginning of time. The Lake District of 40 years ago now charms me with its quaintness. My walking tour in the Lancashire slice of the region was slow and reflective, contrasting markedly with what is accomplished now that there

JONTY WILSON, BLACKSMITH AT KIRKBY LONSDALE.

are good roads and reliable cars. The old roads of Lakeland meandered amiably about the landscape. Now the M6 sweeps grandly northwards, through the Lune Gorge and over the heights of Shap to gain Carlisle. A branch road, the A66, carries traffic at speed to Keswick and West Cumbria. Sanity decreed that the route should have been laid out to the north of Skiddaw but, planning being what it is, a few lines on a map sent it through miles of prime National Parkscape, crossing the Greta on a concrete bridge formed into a gigantic rainbow-arch. The heart of Lakeland is traversed by yet another mighty branch of the M6 – the Kendal bypass, leading into a much-improved road to Windermere. It takes on the proportions of an urban highway when it is not far from Dove Cottage at Grasmere, swaggering up Dunmail Raise towards Thirlmere and Keswick, no doubt making Old Dunmail spin in his grave with irritation at this violation of his old haunts.

To William Wordsworth and his cronies, it was desirable to have a spell in the Wilderness before reaching the Promised Land. So, when they could, they crossed the Sands of Morecambe Bay. Such an excursion was proof of good taste. Wordsworth wrote: "The stranger, from the moment he sets foot upon these Sands, seems to leave the turmoil and traffic of the world behind him; and, crossing the majestic plain when the sea has retired, he beholds, rising apparently from its base, the cluster of mountains among which he is going to wander, and towards whose recesses, by the vale of Conistone, he is gradually and peacefully led".

Lakeland was already besmirched by industry. The remains of bloomeries (iron furnaces) pock-marked the woods and shoreline of the Coniston area known to the Poet. The lake itself was used as a highway for the passage of boats laden with copper ore, slate, flags, birch brooms and small timber. Fishing had greatly declined since the days when the monks of Furness kept a boat of 20 nets there. It would appear that the works of nature and the works created by man were, in Wordsworth's day, on a point of balance. Before long, man would have the upper hand.

We live in a noisy world. For example, traffic on the M6 is loud enough to drown the fell-going farmer's whistled instructions to his dogs. Express trains pass through the Lune Gorge at over 100 miles an hour. Low-flying jets gavort about the district. A farmer of the upper Lune told me, with justifiable exaggeration: "I was sitting on a hay bale in the meadow when one 'plane nearly took me with it!" He added: "Life's all of a splutter!" The last time I walked on the Fairfield Horseshoe, was on a wild Sunday afternoon in winter. Few ramblers were astir and the dominant sounds were the ravens playing hide-and-seek in the mist, or flicking on their backs through the sheer joy of life. It was just like old times! Another day, in Grasmere, the sky held the whine and whoosh of low-flying military jets. I saw one aircraft pass under a flock of 200 startled grey gecsc that had risen from the lake near Waterhead. The aircraft then went wall-hopping up Dunmail Raise. A jet's progress can be frightening, except to sheep, which appear to have grown accustomed to the noise. Local people wince and worry. Two RAF Tornadoes collided near Penrith in August, 1988. Four aircrew died in that incident.

Happily, some of the flavour of old Lakeland remains. Natural beauty abounds. At the head of Ullswater, the fells appear to spring directly from the water, as they do in the fjords of Norway. During the slow progress of the seasons, the colours – always soft – impress by their variety. The lake shore shrugs off winter and puts on a display of snowdrops, followed by the fresh yellow of daffodils – the Wordsworth daffodils, since it was by Ullswater that William and his sister Dorothy saw the flowers that "danced" in the breeze. Daffodils merge with the gold of dead bracken. Soon the beech buds provide a film of green in native woodland on the lower slopes of the fells. A visitor then sees woods that arc misty with bluebells. By early summer, the

ISAAC COOKSON, OF HELTON, NEAR HAWESWATER.

bracken is unfolding, each frond being like a bishop's crozier. Foxgloves – thousands of foxgloves – add a regal shade to the scene.

I collect folk tales. The Vicar of St. Mary's, Applethwaite (an old name for part of what is now Windermere) told me of a Lakeland church at which the clock stopped ticking. Inquiries were made. It was discovered that some 30 years before, a member of the congregation had agreed to wind up the clock weekly. The clock stopped ticking because the old chap had died. Many a Lakelander has gone to the grave taking with him or her some fascinating folk tales. One of the pleasures of editing a Lakeland magazine for 40 years was to record many such stories. *Changing Lakeland* is made up mainly of anecdotes. I heard from Jacob Jackson, verger at Langdale Church for 38 years, how Braithwaite Canon, a local man, "unseated" five members of Parliament. "He were takkin' 'em in a dog cart to Windermere station. There were three at t'back, two at t'front – three wi' 'im. Their weight forced t'shafts up. They were tipped out!"

Everyone told with gusto about changes in the cost of living. In the mid-1920s, coal was delivered to one Cumberland farm at £1.13s a ton and paraffin cost 6d (5p) a gallon. S.H. Cole, of Caldbeck, bought a pair of strong country-made clogs for 8s 6d – a child's clogs cost 5s (25p) – and he paid £1.5s for a pair of first-class shoes. "You could buy a set of caulkers (sole and heel irons) for 8d, with a palmful of clog nails 'thrown in'". In the Newlands Valley, Eardley Swainson had a tale to tell of collecting "coals" from the railway station at Braithwaite. "I'd take a ten bob note (50p). I'd pick up and pay for 10 or 11 cwt of coal and still have some change. I thought more of threepence then than a chap does of ten bob now". No facts about this old way of life were too trivial to be recorded. I watched a Langdale man lime-washing the outside walls of his farmhouse and heard that "a bit o' cow dung, mixed in with lime, helps it to stick better". Limewash was used because it permitted a building to breathe. "Modern paint clogs it up". Down at Rydal, instead of white the favourite shade for the exteriors of houses was yellow ochre.

Jonty Wilson, the Kirkby Lonsdale blacksmith, was unhappy at the passing of what he called "oral traditions". He said that there had been more changes in national life in the past 100 years than in the previous 1,000 years. "Crafts, skills, tools, dialect words, have become obsolete and meaningless now. The horse world and old husbandry have disappeared, passing into the limbo of history ..." So, too, have many of the Lakelander's vivid expressions. At Penruddock, an old man remarked: "I've one foot in t'grave an' t'other foot on a banana skin, ready for slipping in". Wilf Nicholson, of Ambleside, told me of the campers who complained to a farmer that the site he had allocated them was too steep for tents. He pointed at the fells and remarked: "It's like this, lads – God gave us so much ground we had to pile it up in grey big heaps". At Cunniston (Coniston), I asked a veteran his precise age. He said: "I'se eighty-three". Seeking to flatter him, I said: "But you don't look eighty-three". He promptly replied: "Can't help that!" I asked Fred Barker, of Norn Bank, Patterdale, his age. Fred promptly bounced the question back. He invited me to guess what that age might be. I suggested sixty-five. "Nay", said Fred, his eyes twinkling, "I'm varra near a hundred". Eventually, I beat him down to 73, a figure that was confirmed by his wife!

The fell farmers are still a race apart, being in the world but curiously detached from many of its modern aspects. The dalehead families are marvellously self-contained. Not for them the crowds and bright lights. The men are still pre-occupied with sheep, with Herdwicks and Swardles (Swaledales). They endure without self-pity the worst that the weather can give and they stagger through an unbearably long winter – a winter which from a stock-keeping point of

Lakeland Faces. Left – Two men from the Newlands Valley, near Keswick. They are John Tracey, (above, left) a roadman and Eardley Swainson, farmer (left). Pictured above is Bob Casson, who for many years was connected with the "Raven", one of the yacht-like craft that operates a passenger service on Ullswater, between Glenridding and Pooley Bridge.

view is only half over in February, when townsfolk are looking for signs of spring.

Sixty years ago, when there were still many horses to be seen in Lakeland, and men spoke about them with all the enthusiasm now reserved for motor vehicles, blacksmiths were numerous and the maintenance of a horse was proportionally cheaper than is a car today. In the 1920s, having a horse shod with four new shoes cost 9s 6d. A "remove" (the taking off of shoes, dressing of feet and replacement of shoes) was done for 3s 6d. The thrifty farmer ensured that horseshoes lasted longer in summer by fitting "cogs" (blunt metal pegs). In winter, when the roads were slape (slippery), the blacksmith hammered little spikes called "sharps" into the holes on a shoe so that the horse could keep its feet on a smooth surface.

A farmer who was travelling on a motorised trike with "balloon" tyres and a Japanese trademark, taking food "pellets" and hay to his older yows, observed that the sheep knew his daily routine well. They had been watching out for him; they crowded round the trike and followed him eagerly as he left a trail of nutritious food pellets along the fellside pasture. I commented on the "tameness" of modern sheep and recalled their flighty nature in times past. He held up one of the pellets and said this was the reason for the change of manner. He added: "It's powerful stuff – you could tame lions with it!"

Food served to the farm men 40 years ago was cheap and provided staying power. A Langdale farm man said: "In the morning we ate porridge. They set the pan in the middle of the table and you could help yourself. We also had havercake (based on oatmeal). Tea was much too expensive, but the farmers would make coffee. The coffee pot was emptied once a week and egg shells popped in to clean it! At dinner-time, there'd be plenty o' taties and some milk. There were no *cooks* in them days. Farmers' wives were the worst cooks in the world. They'd get a great lump o' meat, boil it for Sunday, and we'd have it cold for the rest of the week. At tea-time there'd be oatcake and slices of white bread. Pastry didn't come along very frequently".

Talk about the weather was the first topic in any Lakeland conversation. A visitor to Seathwaite Farm, the wettest inhabited house in England, inquired: "Does it always rain?" and was told: "Nay – it sometimes snaws (snows)". Meeting T.D. Walshaw in Long Sleddale I heard how his interest in the local rainfall developed about 1950. Being away from the valley during the week, he used a bucket as a gauge and it would be sufficient for a week's rain, yet on several occasions, when he returned home, he found his monster gauge had overflowed. From the records he kept meticulously, it is clear that Longsleddale is one of the wettest places in Westmorland, with an annual average fall of some 100 inches. The period from September to November is usually very wet. At times when there is torrential rain on the "tops", the river Sprint can rise five feet in about half-an-hour. In 1947, snow drifted to the heads of the doors at Sadgill Farm, where the Fishwick family was "blocked in" for nine weeks. "The sheep were cut off in bunches; we could not easily get at them". At Pooley Bridge, Miss Elizabeth Thompson – whose father had a naval career, followed by the captaincy of steamboats on Windermere, then Ullswater – showed me "Admiral Fitzroy's Barometer", which was said to be over a century old. On it was written: "At sunset, a rosy sky presages fine weather; a sickly greenish hue, wind and rain. An Indian red tint, rain. A grey sky, fine weather. A red sky, bad weather".

Changing Lakeland is copiously illustrated because "still" photography enables us to fix vivid images in our minds. We take photography for granted now, but I was to meet Frank Herbert, of Bowness, who started work for the family firm in 1904. The Herberts set up as photographers in the 1880s, when cameras were a novelty and the "wet plate" system in regular use. Photographic plates had to be sensitised on the spot and developed while still wet after being

IN THE PARLOUR OF A PATTERDALE FARM.

exposed. Use was made of a portable lightproof tent, which stood on a tripod. Exposures of several minutes duration were common. The smallest plate used was eight inches by six inches, but the more usual sizes were 12 × 10 or even 15 × 12. No facilities existed for enlargement; the subject had to be photographed at the size needed on the finished print. An old 15 × 12 camera was still owned by the Herbert family when I called to see them. Frank recalled that when he was a small boy in the winter of 1894-5, Windermere was frozen from end to end and 100,000 people ventured on to the ice. This was an exciting subject for the camera of the Herberts, who promptly joined the crowd. The ice was nine inches thick. A coach and four was driven on it. When printing photographs, sensitised paper was placed in frames behind the plates and exposed to the sunlight for a long time. "If there was no sun, the job seemed to last all day. It didn't really matter, though. Time was not so pressing then ..."

Having used a tape-recorder for many years, I have a fine collection of Lakeland voices. John Peel of Lowther told me about the Yellow Earl. When John retired as chief accountant of the Lowther estate in 1966, generous tributes were paid to his 50 years' association with the estate. This John Peel was a descendant of the John Peel of Lakeland hunting fame. "He was a fine old Cumbrian ... A small-time statesman. He doubtless lived more for hunting than for his little farm. He drank – there's no doubt about that. But he was no better, no worse than others of his class and time". Conversation quickly turned to the Yellow Earl – to Hugh Cecil, 5th Earl of Lonsdale. John Peel was at a loss to understand just how the nickname came into use. It is said to have sprung from the fact that the Earl possessed yellow carriages, but such a colour had been in use by the Lonsdales for years before his time. Could "Yellow Earl" have been derived from Hugh's sandy hair? "He was a fine, big, healthy-looking man, full of life and vigour", John recalled. "No one remained in any doubt about his status. You knew immediately that he was someone special ... Normally, his voice was soft, but he could roar like a lion if someone did anything that displeased him. He was a kindly man. He had no family of his own, and both he and her ladyship took a fancy to my daughter. I can remember the Earl arriving outside our home on ponyback and putting the pony through all sorts of little tricks for her delight".

When John Peel became the accountant in 1932, he was summoned to the castle, arriving promptly at 11 a.m. and using the back door, of course. He was then conducted through the magnificent building, along wide stone passages, through rooms decked with fine furnishings and paintings. At the entrance to the Earl's study were two stuffed huskies, a reminder of the Earl's jaunt into the North American Arctic. Animal rugs decked the floor. Representations of snakes were attached to trellis work. The Earl sat at an enormous desk. "One approached him with a sense of awe".

It was always a joy to hear a Lakeland craftsman talking about his young days, for machines were beginning to replace humans. Among the customs which are now mercly items for the history books is "whipping the cat". It was not a cruel sport, like bull or badger baiting, but a method of working used by those country tailors who went from farm to farm converting lengths of cloth into garments. This became known as "whipping the cat". The tailor himself was Tommy or Johnny Whipcat. James William Holt of Bassenthwaite village told me about the craft. At the age of 15 – when a man's suit cost about £2.50 – he became apprenticed to Mr. Harriman Smallwood.

Lakeland farmers sent for the tailors, and during their stay at the farms they were provided with board and lodging. Occasionally, a farmer would arrive with horse and trap to collect the cumbersome sewing machine. "My uncle and I once set out for Millstone Moor, about nine

LOWTHER RED STAGS IN SUMMER AND AUTUMN.

miles away. We carried our tools, including a very heavy iron. The farmer, Tom Allinson, should have met us with the horse and trap. I don't know if he slept in or he couldn't catch the horse, but we walked to Isel School, six miles from home, before we met him". At Thornthwaite Hall Farm, Mr. Holt was faced with a heap of worn clothing and the materials with which to repair them. "It took me from Monday morning until a quarter to four on Saturday to get through it".

A journeyman tailor was paid the equivalent of 12p a day and normally he did well for food. "We got 15s (75p) for cutting and making a suit, and sometimes we had to wait until the following Whitsuntide or Martinmas before we were paid ... There was plenty of work in making a suit, especially if the coat had 10 pockets, the type demanded by a local vet. He wanted two breast, ticket, hip, inside and hare pockets. There were 20 pockets in the whole suit!" Women's clothes were made at Bassenthwaite. The long skirts had a brush braid round the hem to prevent the cloth wearing as it came into contact with the ground. Fabrics were smoothed by "goose" irons weighing between 13lb and 16lb. These had to be heated in a fire that was kept big, otherwise the huge irons would have put it out!"

When I was not chatting with people, I looked for those "other residents" of Lakeland – the birds and mammals, ranging in size from the goldcrest of the fir woods to the red stag of the high fell. Lakeland is small but its woods astonishingly varied, and so is the wildlife. Ernest Bleazard was Keeper of Natural History at Tullie House, Carlisle. I often called for chats about the Lakeland fauna. Ernest was born at Greenodd but his family moved to Carlisle when he was a child; he used to go off and live a tramp's life. "After a day on the fells, I'd seek out a lonely sheep farm and ask for a night's lodging. Or, I'd settle down in an outbuilding to sleep". He never had a car, using public transport, a bicycle or Shank's Pony. Of the fell-top birds he told me that for him the raven best reflected the spirit of high and lonely places. "It's a hardy resident with a gruff voice – one of the few British birds that begin nesting in the winter season and occasionally having eggs in February, even when the fells are covered with snow".

In my experience, few naturalists like sheep, comparing them with goats in the desert. The incessant champing of a large number of sheep can reduce heather ridges to expanses of useless Nardus grass and healthy woodland to a collection of a few geriatric trees, with heavily-cropped areas in between. Yet the sheep are on the hills by the right of 1,000 generations. (I acknowledge that too many sheep will quickly debase a countryside). Tales were told of sheep that ranged the big State forests and were missed out on the seasonal "gathers". These sheep, untouched by hand, had reverted to the wild.

Grizedale Forest, east of Coniston Water, exists primarily to produce first-class timber. The Forestry Commission also developed Grizedale as a place for public enjoyment and, because trees do not grow in a vacuum, they encourage thereby the establishment of a community of wild birds and beasts. In the early 1970s, early morning walkers in the forest must have been startled when they heard curious popping and hissing noises – the sounds made in the grey dawn by an amorous cock capercaillie, the largest grouse in the world. A stock of "capers" had been introduced to Grizedale by the head forester, Bill Grant, who knew the species in his native Scotland and felt they would do well in an area where Scots pine (which provides the capercaillie with its staple diet) had reached a respectable age. The big birds had soon vanished from this, their only, English haunt.

The neglect of native woodland over many years is being remedied by fencing and planting with broadleafed species of trees. The National Trust – which owns about a quarter of the Lake

ABOVE: A SCOTTISH EAGLET. BELOW: A HORSE USED FOR TIMBER EXTRACTION AT THIRLMERE.

District National Trust – plants about 50,000 trees a year. Towards the end of 1988, some 2,000 mixed deciduous trees – oak, ash, birch, rowan and sycamore – were introduced to ground behind Taw House Farm in Eskdale. It was the last major piece of work underaken under a Community Programme Scheme. Members and supporters of the Trust, under the guidance of the Regional Forester, planted 1,000 sessile oaks at Spika Coppice, near Hawkshead. The trees occupy land recently clear-felled of its massed conifers. What a glorious transformation!

Sessile oak is the species that gives Borrowdale its special greenwood appearance. Most of Lakeland must once have been like this. To saunter along the path by the Derwent ("oak river") in the early morning; to see everything as damp, green and mysterious as an Amazonian jungle, is an experience to savour. Early morning ensures that one walks alone; when the sun gets up, the area is no less lovely – now, indeed, the river itself is tinted bright green – but the sense of mystery has gone. Some of the oaks thrive in unpromising circumstances. Trees have wrapped their roots around boulders or have developed from acorns that became lodged in clefts of rock. It is possible to clamber over rocks and look on to the woodland canopy with, in season, the clusters of ripe acorns that normally would ensure the continuation of the woodland. All too often, browsing by animals prevents the natural regeneration.

The Nature Conservancy Council has classified these Borrowdale woods as "clearly in the first echelon of Grade 1 sites". Until the turn of the century, the area was coppice and provided raw material for many a woodland industry. Borrowdale was once noted for its hazels – its "little nut-trees" – but when man no longer clear-felled the wood the oaks became dominant. Plantations of larch trees appeared. Now the Great Wood of Borrowdale is being rejuvenated and The National Trust has planted 3,500 oaks and Scots pine. In addition, 200 mixed broadleafed trees have been introduced to the scree at Raven Crag, Langdale, to help stabilise the scree. Workers on this arid, shifting slope had to transport soil as well as young trees.

The National Park Authority's woodland estate extends to 488 hectares of broadleaved woods, of which 250 hectares lie in the Rusland Valley. To the south of Rusland are the wooded heights of Haverthwaite, acquired in 1987 with financial assistance from the Countryside Commission and the World Wildlife Fund. It is a hopeful story.

THESE WALKERS are crossing Crinkle Crag, at the head of Great Langdale. Fell-walking has grown in popularity to such an extent that it is rare to be able to walk on grass. The boots of thousands of visitors have stripped away the vegetation, also the underlying peat, exposing the bedrock, which itself is becoming marked by boots. Farmers who could once rely on their sheep finding a useful bite of grass on the ridges now shake their heads at the sight of extensive erosion. Some of the Lakeland paths are now visible, on a clear day, to walkers on the Pennines.

The National Trust is among those who are giving high priority to the maintenance and repair of footpaths. The system adopted on steep ground is called "pitching", which involves cutting a channel and inserting a stone like an iceberg, with only its tip showing. Stones are laid side by side, rather like building a wall on the ground. The cracks are filled with loose material and then scattered with grass seed.

These and other techniques have halted erosion in a number of popular places, such as Stickle Gill in Langdale, Helm Crag near Grasmere and Sour Milk Gill, leading up from Seathwaite at the head of Borrowdale. Walkers are pleased to follow such paths in preference to slithering on soil or making an ankle-cracking passage on scree to and from the skyline. Some sections of footpaths have been re-routed along less steep gradients to reduce damage to the landscape.

IN HIGH PLACES

NORMAN NICHOLSON wrote a poem about walking walls. My main lament is that now the fells themselves are walking. Battalions of visitors who stagger up the slopes and ramble along the airy ridges are returning to their cars with their big boots clagged with Lakeland soil and pebbles. Each year, the fells are being eroded and fractionally re-modelled. The daring young man who descends from Gable by slithering on a scree slope is causing as much erosion in five minutes as would occur naturally, through wind, rain, frost and thaw, in a matter of five years.

Mountains were feared and avoided. Then, early last century, partly through the influence of writings by such as Christopher North and the Lake Poets, they developed an appeal for those with a sense of adventure. In due course, the most difficult route to the summit was chosen. Minor miracles were achieved on crag faces by men and some women wearing nailed boots on their feet and carrying hempen ropes. They were emulating an Ennerdale shepherd, J. Atkinson, who in 1826, with courage and skill, climbed Pillar Rock by the west route. In the 1920s, boots began to give way to plimsolls, which were more sensitive, followed in post-war days by shoes fitted with "Commando" soles.

Stanley Watson of Borrowdale, and Jim Cameron, who lived at Coniston, were two men I met who had tales to relate from the point of view of experienced climbers deriving part of their income from tuition in the techniques of rock climbing. Stanley had some assistants. I asked him why people climb. He regarded the sport as a type of madness; a tempting of Providence not in accordance with "safety first". But to the cragsman, finally perched above the world like an eagle, triumphant from a struggle with his bare hands, comes a wild joy of mastery; of independence and aloofness – a sense of self-sufficiency, elemental and perhaps barbaric, but extraordinarily thrilling and indescribably satisfying.

Stanley told me of the outspoken pupil who asked an assistant: "What happens if the rope breaks?" The assistant replied: "Don't worry about that, sir. We've plenty more ropes at home". Jim had seen two lads scrambling about the crags of the Old Man. Those lads moved with the verve of mountain goats and seemed indifferent to the danger. One of them remarked: "If we go on like this, we'll be good enough to use ropes!" Jim led the Coniston Mountain Rescue Team which, formed in 1948, was the first of its type in the Lake District. A group that began with 15 members once went out five times in a 10-day spell. When celebrating its 40th birthday at the *Sun Inn,* Coniston, a call-out was received. The 40 members put down their knives and forks and went to help a man who had been hit by a falling tree.

The chatter of a helicopter's rotor blades and the sight of a yellow-painted machine hovering over the fells, about to airlift an injured walker or climber to hospital, remind me of a meeting with the RAF Mountain Rescue Unit almost 30 years ago. This energetic team, one of the most exclusive in the Service, has an arm badge featuring two ice axes on a coil of rope. The first helicopters to appear were *Whirlwinds,* replaced by *Sea Kings* in 1979. In this first year of

Above: *Erica Lindsay Murray holds a sculpture of Haskett Smith, a climbing pioneer. The sculpture is shown close up (above). Below – Dungeon Ghyll Hotel, in Great Langdale.*

operation, based at Boulmer, they were used in Lakeland on 18 occasions. Joe Boothroyd, giving his chairman's report for the Mountain Rescue Teams in 1982, mentioned "non mountain incidents". These went from one extreme to another, from the recovery of personnel and equipment from old mine workings to the safe return of a near grown peregrine falcon chick to its nest on the sea cliffs of West Cumbria. "The involvement of Mountain Rescue Teams in water sport rescue is noted this year, as is the recovery of pilots of flying machines of different types, from jets to hang gliders".

I have seen rock climbers at close quarters while following the higher paths on Great Gable. At Westmorland Cairn, I settle down for a view of Wasdale, with a blue lake lapping and fretting far below, and think of a member of the Westmorland family, "Rusty", whom I met at Threlkeld. He was the son of Thomas Westmorland, a Penrith leather manufacturer. When I last spoke to him, "Rusty" was 86 years old, with failing eyesight, yet he was going on to the fells three times a week, and excitedly contemplated taking a ski-ing holiday in Norway during the following spring. "Rusty" was in the Army for 32 years, being invalided out in 1944. His home was shadowed by Blencathra, over which – he told me – he had walked in the 1890s. When he was eight years old he had been taken up Cross Fell by his father and sister, an expedition that taught him something about "false crests". That same year, he strode along Striding Edge to gain the summit of Helvellyn.

Lakeland had many such characters. At Grasmere, Timmy (Timothy) Tyson repaired shoes and clogs. When he was four years old, his mother took him from Irton (where he was born) over Muncaster Fell end to Waberthwaite, to be measured for some shoes by Moses Dodgson. New snow covered the route and at one stage, they were lost. Timmy moved to Grasmere in 1904; he retained his love of the high hills, climbing virtually all of them – and having a swim in every Lakeland tarn!

In 1951, while walking in Kentmere, I met 78-year-old R.P. Sisson, a Kendalian who built Garth Nest as a retirement home but was often away – on foot. "My ambition years ago was to tramp every square mile of Westmorland and I've pretty well done it". In old age, he could walk 15 miles and think nothing of it. In his prime, he covered 38 miles on a Sunday. He was one of a trio capable of walking 50 miles in a day. One Sunday morning they left Kendal at 5 a.m. and walked through Crook to the Ferry. They rowed across the lake, walked on to High Sawrey and Hawkshead, then over Tarn Hows to Coniston, climbing Coniston Old Man (and being at the top by 1.30 p.m.). After a good meal at Coniston, they continued to the Langdales and Ambleside, ordering coffee at the *Troutbeck Bridge Hotel*. "It was evening by now, and the third member of the party fell asleep. Billy Ingle and I got him between us and set off for Kendal. We dropped him on his mother's doorstep some time after 1 a.m."

Said Mr. Sisson: "You don't see much of the landscape from those great motor coaches. It's best seen while walking – or from the coach and four that used to operate from the *King's Arms* at Kendal when I was young. One day I took a party by coach to Grasmere to climb Helvellyn. There were ladies in the party. Their hair was "frizzed" and they wore bustles. It might have conformed to the style of the time but was not ideal for rambling!"

Old-time shepherds going to the fell made no special preparations. A man simply picked up a stick, called for his dogs and strode off. He might carry a sandwich or two for dinner. If he did not feel hungry, he'd give the sandwiches to the dogs. Such men had a blow-out (gargantuan meal) at night. The reward for all this effort was slight by modern standards. In the lean 1930s, Herbert Grisedale, of Great Langdale, was asked to do some film work. He had simply to be

Fell-going farmer. Charles Relph, of Ashness Farm, near Keswick. Above – Part of a handsomely-carved shepherd's crook. Below – A Lakeland sheepdog. Pure-bred collies are not always kept.

himself – a farmer working his dog. He was paid £3 a day for two days. "I'd never earned such good money before".

Sheep farmers knew every inch of the fells. In Great Langdale, the Grisedale family, of Middle Fell, ran their sheep on the Pikes. Herbert Grisedale told me: "I went round t'back o' t'Pikes three times a day – twice when shepherding and once at night, when I helped to bring down an injured climber ... Father, my brother and me were up there one day when a thunderstorm broke. Said father: 'Get back home lads, as quickly as possible'. I reached the farm in 11 minutes. My brother was a few minutes longer. Dad – he was no longer "lish" – arrived an hour later, drenched to the skin!"

Leslie Grisedale, who in his early working life had a shepherding job with Harry Blenkhorn, ran his sheep on Shap Fell and recalled the wintry spell of February 1947, when the landscape was "wrapped up" with snow. "We never saw a blade of grass for eight weeks. It was well into March before the hill ends came through again. There was plenty of snow at lambing time". The losses of sheep were heavy, for after the snow came frost, preventing the animals from reaching the herbage. One day, Leslie was swept down the fellside by an avalanche. He had been walking round the crag-edges when the snow broke. "It was a stroke of luck I was on the back of it or it would have packed me up properly. The dogs were with me. We were carried to within 500 yards of the main Shap road".

As a shepherd, Leslie lived at a house standing about 1,000 feet above sea level and half a mile from the next habitation. Coal was delivered periodically. Just before lambing time, he cut peat. The turves were turned about a month later and in the calm spell before haytime were transported to the house. "I liked the peat fire. A lot of people objected to the white dust that peat leaves everywhere in the room, but there's always a bit of dirt in a farmhouse. This peat dust was clean dirt after all!" Tom Dixon, of Forest Hall, on Shap, had a white pony which he entered in a racing event at Selside. One day as the horse was competing, Tom urged it on by shouting in the native speech: "Go it frog-slother (spawn) and bent", an apt description of the countryside that was better known to the white pony than the lush field in which it was now running.

The passes that link the head of one dale to another provide a motorist with a rapid introduction to the high fells. It was within a 20 minute walk of the summit of Wrynose, between Little Langdale and the Duddon, that I saw my first mountain ringlet butterfly, a species that is both scarce and attractive. In the 1930s, prompted by the large number of unemployed, the Cumberland County Council drew up plans for tarmacadaming some of the highest passes. Happily, interest waned or the spare cash ran out before this was carried to completion. Fifty years ago, when Mr. and Mrs. Peter Hodgson moved into Fell Foot, the farmhouse at the head of Little Langdale, Wrynose was little more than a walkers' route. Farmers used it when driving stock to or from the Duddon. Wrynose was an Army training ground between 1939 and 1945 and the Army provided this pass with a durable surface as compensation when they no longer needed to use it with their heavy vehicles.

A crossing from Duddon to Eskdale is possible using Hardknott Pass, the modern story of which was given to me by Joseph Dawson, of Boot, in Eskdale. He had worked on the highways for 43 years and remembered when Hardknott was unmetalled, cared for by the men of Black Hall and Brotherilkeld Farms. "The Council paid them for their trouble", said Joseph. Then a "cloudburst" swept away stretches of the road. "You could have hidden a cow in one of the potholes". Next summer, Joseph and two other men repaired the road and gave it a gravelly

NEAR THE LADSTOCK MINERS' PATH, TOWARDS BRAITHWAITE.

surface. For years, a horse and cart was the heaviest traffic. An old lady from Cockley Beck walked across the pass with baskets of butter for a shop in Boot. When Hardknott was clogged with snow, 16 men worked almost a month to clear the ancient highway. It was, said Joseph, "knocked to bits" in the 1939-45 war when Army vehicles roamed the area. The tarmac was added after the war. For years, snow-cutting teams laboured to keep it open in winter. No one tackles the drifts today. The two passes are normally closed until the snow thaws.

As passes go, Whinlatter is not too severe, nor does it have the fell-top feel of many another pass. It nonetheless made special demands on those who worked on it – men such as Norman Scott, who was employed by Cumberland County Council for 42 years, serving for most of the time on Whinlatter. He could easily recall when the Forestry Commission began to plant up the landscape with conifers, which give to the pass the flavour of the Canadian backwoods. Norman Scott worked on a road that was waterbound, being puddly in wet weather and very dusty when dry. The surface was "metalled" about 1926. "When we were kids, we were so excited when a car came through Lorton on its way to Whinlatter, we'd run through the village to have a good look at it". An old green lane in the area was used for trials involving belt-driven, single gear motor cycles.

Before it was given a durable surface, Whinlatter needed much attention. "At slack times, farmers contracted to cart road material. They got eight shillings a day for horse, cart and man". Norman Scott's first wage, in the 1920s, was 6s 8d a day. Yet, this being a time of industrial depression, he considered himself lucky to have a job. His work began at 7 a.m. The foreman was often "hanging about" to satisfy himself that the men had arrived for work on time. Following the 1947 blizzard, Whinlatter Pass was blocked for six weeks. By day, the men worked by hand to clear the snow. Each night, the cruel wind blew more snow into their excavations.

The road from Ambleside to Kirkstone Pass is known as "The Struggle". A wise motorist engages a low gear for the descent as well as the ascent, the maximum gradient being 1 in 3½. As you journey upwards, climbing 1,300 feet in three miles, you notice a low, white-faced building on what appears to be a ledge cut from living rock. It is the well-named *Travellers' Rest*. Kirkstone Pass reaches an elevation of 1,476 ft and the inn is not quite at the summit. When I first visited the hostelry, I was greeted by a St. Bernard dog named Ajax and saw a framed copy of the *Hiker's Motto:* "Don't look at the hill and grumble – climb it!" The "new" road from Troutbeck lacks the character and age of "The Struggle". It has "A" classification being a grand highway from the Windermere area via Kirkstone and the shores of Brotherswater to Ullswater and Penrith. *The Traveller's Rest,* which was given a licence about 1840, is the third highest inn in England (the highest are *Tan Hill,* on the Durham/Yorkshire border and the *Cat and Fiddle* in Derbyshire).

Being precariously balanced on a lonely fell, Kirkstone's hostelry is the only inn of the three that gives any indication of height above sea level. Mark Atkinson bought the business in 1914. I chatted with his son, Ion, who had become the uncrowned king of Kirkstone, owning most of the land on either side of the road. Ion lived at Syke Side Farm, near Brotherswater, leaving the day-to-day running of the inn to his son-in-law and daughter, Mr. and Mrs. Michael Dand, who told me: "When the wind gets going, you wonder how the house stands up. You can sometimes feel the pressure of air on your ears when you are sitting indoors". I had noticed that the wind had been playing tricks with the television aerial, but an aerial on the skew was still able to receive programmes from Holme Moss, some 90 miles away. I looked down on Windermere and saw the lake surface being ruffled by wind. I was told to brace myself for the coming gust, for a strong wind races by the inn like a tornado. "Last summer", said Michael Dand, "a small car was blown away". Ion mentioned that Pat Leighton, a former postman, was blown over a wall, but the experience did not deter him. He was still delivering the mail on his 81st birthday! In 1914, the mail was being delivered twice a week, on Tuesdays and Saturdays. After the Great War, it was delivered on three days. When, in the early 1930s, the Postmaster General proudly announced that there was not a place in England without a daily delivery, "we took him up on it, and got notice of a daily delivery – by return of post!"

For a great many years, Joseph Gregg drove Herdwick sheep over Wrynose and Hardknott so that they might be displayed at Eskdale Show; he used to set off from Kentmere on Wednesday, the show being on Friday, and he stayed overnight at Elterwater or Little Langdale. Sixty years ago, other sheep-breeders – among them Isaac Thompson, of West Head, Wythburn – were on the passes with sheep. Driving them was a task demanding patience and a good dog. In Eskdale, young Joseph Gregg stayed at the *Woolpack*. If there was no room at the inn, he "kipped" where he could, sometimes snuggling down in the "brackens" on the fellside. He was in Eskdale one year when he received a telegram from his brother to say that he must return home immediately to deliver 400 half-bred lambs from Kentmere to Kendal station for 4 p.m. on Saturday. He started walking from the *Woolpack* about 10.30 p.m. and was at Kentmere Hall, ready to muster the sheep, at 5 a.m. In 1908, he took 90 draft ewes to Ambleside Fair, his instructions being to get 11s apiece for them. The best bid was 9s, so he drove the sheep home; they were eventually sold for 13s each.

Among those who have achieved celebrity status in Lakeland is Chris Bonington, the author of many books dealing with expeditions to the highest mountains in the world. Chris, who has for many years lived in a converted farmhouse "back o' Skiddaw", first came to the Lakes in the mid-1950s, until which time his experience of British mountains was confined to North Wales. Married to Wendy in 1962, he launched himself on a freelance career associated with mountaineering. They have special memories of their first home, "a loft in a barn near Loughrigg. We had just one room; it was very grotty, with no amenities at all". Several homes later, Chris and Wendy moved to Manchester, to be nearer the centre of things. "Then we decided that we really did like living in the Lakes; we moved back up here and I cannot see us moving again". The nearest crags are in Borrowdale.

He spends several months each year away from home, but Lakeland is ever in his mind. Chris told me: "I love the Lakes. The area is as beautiful as anywhere in the world. There is no feeling of anti-climax when I get home; it's the very reverse – a feeling of excitement". He thinks that man's impact has actually enhanced the beauty in the dales. "Lakeland farmhouses are extraordinarily beautiful places. The architecture so blends with the landscape that you feel the farms – and the people – truly belong. You feel, indeed, that you are part of a great tradition".

Harry Griffin, a journalist who has written millions of words about the Lake District, and who has spent a considerable part of his leisure time above the 1,500 ft contour lines, grew up at Barrow-in-Furness. I last met Harry when he was 76 years of age. He still reckoned to go on at least 100 fell-going excursions a year. To wander around Cunswick End, his home near Kendal – as I did in 1986 – was to have a feeling of a house turned inside out. Pictures and artefacts related to the great outdoors. In his study, Harry handed me a stone axe head he had picked up in Langdale. I saw RSPCA medallions awarded to him for rescuing sheep from ledges

*RUNNING ON
THE "TOPS"*

The name of Bill Teasdale, of Caldbeck, is respected wherever fell-runners gather. Above – The "tape" is raised for Bill on completing a Grasmere guides' race. Right – The champion as he is today. He sportingly returned to a competitive event, after a long retirement, for the benefit of television cameras. He ran a worthy race.

– one from Whitbarrow Scar and another for Rainsborrow Crag. Above the fireplace in the drawing room was a painting by an old friend, W. Heaton Cooper.

Harry showed me a photograph of himself leading a climb on Dow Crag 55 years before. "I was practically brought up on Dow Crag", he said. He wore corduroy knee breeches, nailed boots ("they were nailed with clinker nails") and black plimsolls, if the holes in the rock were too small or the crag was dry. The plimsolls, purchased from Woolworths at 10d a pair, had a criss-cross pattern on the sole. "The idea was to get them one size too small so that your feet were tightly enclosed. You wore them out very quickly – and got another pair. In those days we also used hemp rope".

At Barrow Library, Harry saw books written by rock-climbing pioneers – by Owen Glyn Jones and the Abrahams. He browsed through early numbers of the *Journal* of the Fell and Rock Climbing Club. At the age of 16 years, he cycled the 23 miles from Barrow to a point from which he could admire Coniston Old Man and its neighbours. He was impressed by Dow Crag and by the attendant climbers. "This inspired me to start rock-climbing. But how could I begin when I knew so little about it? The only person I'd heard of who did rock-climbing from Barrow was George Basterfield, one of the pioneers, and a man with a number of first ascents to his credit. At the time he was Mayor of Barrow. I went along to seek an interview with the Mayor and to ask him how I could have my boots fitted with those 'clinker' nails!"

The Mayor told him where at Coniston he could get the special nails. He then announced that he was going to visit Dow Crag on the following Sunday and Harry was welcome to join him. "I could hardly believe my good fortune. On the way, I overtook him; we then walked together to Dow Crag, with George telling me about features in the area". He was observant. Looking at some footprints on the ground, he announced to Harry Griffin that A.T. Hargreaves and Bill Clegg would be on the Crag that day. How did he know? Hargreaves was wearing footwear with a special type of climbing nail he had invented. It left a distinctive mark on the ground.

Harry remembers George Abraham, one of the celebrated brothers who photographically recorded aspects of the golden age of Lakeland climbing. "I was speaking to George shortly before he died. He was then about 93". Harry first climbed Napes Needle when he was 19 years old. We discussed the impending centenary of Haskett Smith's ascent. Harry was once in his company, though he did not actually speak to him. "He was a big man and had a long, Chinese-type moustache. He wore ultra large clothes and was very scruffy".

Harry was one of nine young men who formed a group and acquired the first climbing hut in the Lake District. "It was a wooden shed, almost like a garage, and it stood in a field at Coniston Old Hall. We spent many week-ends there. We had a ritual of having a dip in Coniston Water or Goats Water on each excursion.

Over 30 years have gone by since I first chatted with W. Heaton Cooper, the artist. I recall the conversation mainly because, when asked about Lakeland weather, he said: "I never think of 'good' days or 'bad' days. There are 'dry' days and 'wet' days. I can get pleasure from each". Not so long ago, I asked him when he began serious rock-climbing. He replied: "I'm afraid it was never serious. It was always fun. I started rock-climbing with my brothers and sisters, before my tenth birthday. We were born at the foot of a very craggy mountain, Coniston Old Man. That was our playground. We played on rocks as a quite normal activity".

Heaton Cooper, at the age of 83, was the subject of a BBC television film, "Rock and Running Water", the first full-length programme about "The People's Painter", a man whose output has been so prolific that he has no idea how many paintings he has completed. Each year,

LOOKING EAST, across Bassenthwaite Lake, our solitary walker sees, on the lower slopes of the fells that culminate in Skiddaw, the evidence of dense conifer forests. The Forestry Commission has planted extensively in Lakeland. Early efforts were denounced as being totally out of keeping with the beauty and naturalness round about. Then, in 1963, Dame Sylvia Crowe was appointed the Commission's first landscape consultant. She held the position for 13 years.

She was responsible for the shift in attitude from square blocks and harsh lines to irregular shapes and blending forest patterns in sympathy with the landform; these have been the hullmark of the Commission's younger plantations established in the past 20 years. Dame Sylvia, thinking especially of regions like the Lake District and North Wales, with their small-scale contrasts of landform and delicately modelled hills, insisted that every plantation must be treated individually and fitted into the intricate pattern.

Ennerdale Forest, acquired by the Commission in 1926, and in clear view not only from the valley bottom, but also from the peaks, by fell-walkers and climbers, is being redesigned and reshaped, so that it looks more natural than was once the case.

Cold water from the "tops". The Beck from Rachell Fell flows above "Seldom Seen", near Thornthwaite.

10,000 prints of his work and 70,000 greetings cards depicting his scenes are purchased at the studio in Grasmere. The television film brought out the essence of the painter. He works from a spiritual conviction inspired by the natural beauty of the area.

He told me that when he was 15, having read much about climbing, he travelled to Keswick and bought a pair of strong boots. "They were farmer's boots, with big nails and 'caulkers'. Those boots were almost as hard as wood, so I walked from Keswick to Grasmere, where we were then living, along the tops and eased them in. There were a lot of bogs on the way! By the time I got to Grasmere, they were easier to wear – but I was rather tired!" For six years, he climbed by himself. He had no experience of climbing with others, yet when Gordon Osmaston, a Major in the Royal Engineers, came on leave from India – where he was doing survey work – he asked Heaton Cooper if he would show him and a young lady, June Archer, some Lakeland climbs. Heaton Cooper agreed. "I had heard of a crag called Gimmer, but I had never found it. I hadn't a rope, so I went to a farmer friend and borrowed 40 feet of cart rope".

The trio surmounted Middle Fell Buttress with some ease and eventually found Gimmer Crag. "We saw a ledge leading from right to left; it was rising diagonally. We went along this quite easy ledge until we reached the end and then I could see a quite good route above us. (We were already about 150 ft above the foot of the crag). The new route went almost vertically upwards. "We got to a small ledge with an overhang above it. My two companions sat on the ledge while I got a bit farther. I reached an overhang, about 30 or 40 feet away. Not being able to get over it, I came down and unroped. Gordon tried; then he attempted to come down again, but he couldn't reach the ledge we were on. I asked June to sit on my legs, and I lay out over space and said to Gordon: 'jump!' He jumped – and I fielded him!" They regained the safe ledge – Ash Tree Ledge. "It appears that the climb we were attempting is severe and has only been climbed fairly recently. It is considered a very good climb. It's not surprising we didn't get to the top of it".

I asked Heaton Cooper what the average climber was wearing in the 1920s. He said he had not known any average climbers! "I knew what I wore, which was ordinary tweeds and sweater – usually two sweaters". He enjoyed the comradeship of some remarkable men, including Harry Kelly, who had been asked to edit a new set of climbing guides. "He wasn't satisfied with the type of illustrations that had been used in guides; they were photographs and did not reveal the rock in enough detail. A smudge on the photograph could be a juniper bush, a tuft of heather or an overhang. He asked me if I would do him some drawings". The first feature to be so illustrated, in 1935, was Pillar Rock. So successful did this prove that he was asked to continue illustrating new guides, which he did for many years.

In his early days as a climber, he used a bicycle to reach distant crags. Sometimes he would go by bus. "I very often had to run all the way down from Scafell Pike or Scawfell to the 'Old Dungeon Ghyll' to catch the last bus home". He went through a motor-cycle period. "I was so ashamed of the noise the bike made that I soon gave it up. At the time of the Suez crisis I had a scooter, to use less petrol. We were all patriotic. The scooter took me into remote parts of England and Scotland. The first car I got was an Austin 7, which was 10 years old. I got it for £6, and – not knowing how to drive it – I learnt by going out in it!" On his expeditions to the fells, he carried a bag of raisins and dark sugar and took a mouthful now and again when he felt hungry. "Sometimes I took sandwiches, sometimes an onion. I got the idea of eating an onion from a Lakeland huntsman, George Chapman".

Heaton Cooper's real love has been painting, not rock-climbing. "I did rock-climbing for fun. It was nice to make such good friends. I'm really very sad when people take up rock-

Felltop personalities Above, left – *"Rusty" Westmorland, photographed at Troutbeck.* Below, left *Betty Wainwright and A. Wainwright of fell-top guidebook fame.* Above: *Joe Wells, of Martindale, who cared for sheep and red deer.* Below – *Mr. and Mrs Jim Naylor of Wasdale Head.*

climbing in the Lake District as seriously as they do now. Last year, there were 230 first ascents. Some of them were about 40 feet high, which is absolute nonsense. We would not have thought about recording a little bit of rock 40 feet high". We chatted about different attitudes to rock-climbing – about "then" and "now". "There are so many climbs today you couldn't climb free. You've got to use pitons and the rest. I never bothered with them. They didn't appeal to me at all, being more like engineering than fun".

Gimmer Crag remained his favourite crag. "I started climbing there. Also, it's nice and open. Gimmer is 'face-climbing'. I don't like a lot of gullies and chimneys. There's always too much rock. I'd much rather get out on to an open face and trust to my balance rather than pulling up with my arms ..." His final words to me that day were: "I've never been particularly good as a rock-climber – but I've enjoyed the sport enormously".

Most people who venture above the 1,500 feet contour think of Alfred Wainwright and, in particular, his hand-written, hand-drawn guide books to the Lake District fells – a quite original and most useful contribution to the vast library of local books. Wainwright, who was born and bred in urban Lancashire, had a revelation of natural beauty when, on his first visit to Lakeland, he climbed Orrest Head, from which he beheld Windermere and a skyline made up of shapely mountains. With great good fortune, he secured a job in local government at Kendal and began his meticulous exploration of the fells, invariably using public transport to reach the walking areas.

I first met A.W. in the early 1950s. Harry Firth, who printed our magazine *"Cumbria"* at Kendal, showed me the material for the first of the famous guides. It was in the form of pages featuring A.W.'s drawings and miniscule writing. Plates would be made from this art work and the printing would take place directly from those plates; there would be no type to set up. I marvelled at the penmanship. I chuckled at some examples of the author's humour.

When A.W. sat down on the evening of November 9, 1952, to draw the first page of his proposed series of guide books, he was doing the work for his own interest and against the time when he might not be able to stride across the fells. Then he could look at his work and derive pleasure from his store of memories. He was to carry his venture to its breathtaking conclusion at the rate of one page a day – with a little time off twice a week so that he might watch *Coronation Street* on the television; it reminded him of his upbringing in the industrial town of Blackburn. A.W. recalls that his first page dealt with an ascent of Dove Crag. As he did the work, "I was lost to all else".

Maps fascinate him. He soon made the acquaintance of the 2½"-scale, then the 6" maps which provided him with the drystone wall patterns and the courses of old roads and paths, many of which had served mines, quarries and sheepfolds and were now abandoned. He found pleasure in trying to evoke the scenes of former human activity. "Silence is always more profound in places where once there was noise". Not for him the crowds, but "the secret places that must be searched for, the drove roads and neglected packhorse trails, the ruins of abandoned industries, the adits and levels and shafts of the old mines and quarries, the wild gullies and ravines that rarely see a two-legged visitor". The seven pictorial guides were compiled for his own pleasure in the years from 1952 to 1965, "both years inclusive, as the buff forms say". He has never changed his style, "and if I were starting all over again, I would not change a thing".

The books have made a great deal of money, though when I called to see Wainwright in his treasurer's office in Kendal Town Hall at the outset of the scheme he had not drawn a penny and had incurred a printers' debt of over £900. Most of the royalties have gone to his favourite charity, a Cumbrian animal rescue centre. He is deeply moved by the plight of straying or abandoned animals and is delighted that something has been done in Cumbria to alleviate the distress. He says: "When I walked the fells, animals were my own companions. They had an uncomplaining acceptance of the conditions in which they lived – out in dreadful weather all the time".

A.W. has planned on his death to have his ashes scattered on Haystacks, in the western fells. To him, Haystacks is "the best fell-top of all, a place of great charm and fairy tale attractiveness ..." He concluded his *Fellwanderer* book with the words: "And if you, dear reader, should get a bit of grit in your boot as you are crossing Haystacks in the years to come, please treat it with respect. It might be me".

AFLOAT IN LAKELAND

EVEN THE major lakes change. They were created when glaciers deepened old river valleys and when the melting ice left natural dams called moraines. Wastwater and Ennerdale are the two least changed of the lakes and hold little life. There is a blueness about Wastwater even on warm summer days, yet Windermere, set in a pastoral and well populated area, has a rich planktonic bloom at this time. The most changed of the major lakes is Esthwaite Water. Nearly half its drainage area has been cultivated and it has for many years received the run-off from farming and human activity.

Some Lakeland tarns – including the celebrated Tarn Hows – came into being through industrial activity, when water power was in vogue. The water needs of urban areas were met by damming up some of the "meres" and "waters" of Lakeland, converting them into reservoirs with unsightly shorelines. Ennerdale has helped to fill the water cisterns of the coastal communities. Thirlmere is connected to the taps of Manchester. Even Windermere and Ullswater have been tapped by civic authority, though in such a way that the works are not intrusive.

The most glamorous boats that cruised on Windermere can be seen at the Steamboat Museum just to the north of Bowness. The Museum was opened by the Prince of Wales in May, 1977. A representative collection of craft evokes the spirit of late Victorian and Edwardian times. Then the folk who had become rich from transactions in cotton and shipping built homes overlooking Windermere. Luxury and elegance, so evident on dry land, were also to be found on the lake, where pleasant hours were spent on board small steamboats. These became the status symbols of late Victorian times and were cherished by people who found pleasure in novelty. The Victorians were great innovators. Ordinary folk, having travelled to Windermere by rail, used the steamers operated by the Furness Railway Company.

To list the objects to be found at the Steamboat Museum would be to invite writer's cramp. My own favourite is also the oldest – Dolly, carvel built, 41ft long. She operated on Windermere for nearly 40 years and was then transported, probably on horse-drawn timber wagon to Ullswater. The boat sank in 1895. And there she remained, forgotten, until divers saw her in 1960. They swam up to her and were confronted by a lovely funnel; they noticed that the cabin windows retained their glass. She was raised and prepared for public viewing.

George Pattinson once invited me to join him for a cruise in the *Esperance*. He first told me something of the story of this famous iron-hulled craft, which through the vivid imagination of Arthur Ransome became the houseboat of "Swallows and Amazons". *Esperance* was built by T.B. Seath and Company of Rutherglen in 1869, being conveyed in sections to be re-assembled on the shore of Windermere. Her owner was H.W. Schneider, the Furness industrialist. When she steamed into Bowness Bay that summer, almost the whole village turned out to watch her. Men who were familiar with boats were impressed when told she had twin screws.

She carried Schneider from Belsfield, his mansion overlooking Bowness Bay, to the station at Lakeside, seven miles away by lake transport. A special train then conveyed him to business at Ulverston or Barrow. (After parting from his family each morning, Schneider walked down to the *Esperance* pier, preceded, it is said, by his butler, who carried breakfast set out on a silver tray. The meal was eaten as the craft furrowed the waves. It would take the boat rather less than an hour to reach Lakeside).

After Schneider's death, the *Esperance* was left high and dry in a literal sense. Then she was purchased by Mr. Logan, of the *Ferry Hotel,* to be used on the journey to Bowness. Guests at the hotel also used her to attend church at Wray. Even when her engines had been removed at the end of the 1914-18 war, she kept her dignity, for she was commended to the world as the houseboat in some of Ransome's Lakeland tales. Just before the 1939-45 war, *Esperance* lay in 20 feet of water, but local people still recalled her as the "grand old lady" of Windermere. The Pattinson family had her raised before irreparable harm was caused to the interior panelling.

On the day I sailed in her, the funnel was taking exhaust fumes from her two 4-cylinder Ford engines. There was lamentation at Windermere when the original engines were removed. We left the moorings at Rayrigg Bay and cruised on the lake, under the power of one engine. George Pattinson took me to the after saloon, which contained photographs of other notable Windermere steamers. Pictured here was the *Fairy Queen,* owned by Col. G.J.M. Ridehalgh, of Fellfoot, and like the *Esperance* built at Rutherglen. A second photograph was of the *Banshee,* owned by Sir William Forwood and launched in 1882. It was in the forward saloon that George Pattinson afterwards entertained me to tea. Once more the *Esperance* was moored in Rayrigg Bay. I could hear wavelets licking their lips against her iron hull.

On my first crossing of Windermere by ferry, in 1952, the boat was coal-powered and the ticket was issued by Jack Bowman, of Windermere, who had been in charge of the service since 1937. As now, cables kept the boat to a fixed path across the water between a point south of Bowness (Westmorland) and the *Ferry Hotel,* which then stood in Lancashire. Five hundredweights of coal were incinerated every day to activate the 12 h.p. engine. The ferry service drew great loyalty from Joss Hartley who had been driving the ferry for a quarter of a century, and James Sharpe, the relief driver, employed for a decade. When the ferry had grounded on shingle – which the crew kept immaculate, using a rake – I strode to Far Sawrey and heard from John Hoggarth of the days when the ferry service was maintained by a rowing boat, manned by four men. When horses and carts had to be transported, the horses were taken out of their shafts to conserve space.

In his early days on the ferry, Jack Bowman had to deal with livestock being driven in herds or flocks. Sheep, cows, horses, fell ponies: all had to be counted by the ferrymen, the charge in the case of sheep being so much per half dozen. Hearing a clattering of hooves near the *Ferry Hotel,* young Jack Bowman saw a drove of 70 ponies appear, heading for the ferry. Somewhat flustered, he rushed into the cabin and shut the door. The ponies clattered across the deck and fell into the lake. Two farmers – Bruce Rigg and Bruce Logan – were not amused by the sight of their valuable horses swimming in all directions. A cow belonging to John Gibson, who farmed at Sawrey, swam across the lake in preference to using the ferry. When the boat arrived on the Westmorland shore, Jack Bowman chased the cow but discovered it still had plenty of spirit. "It jumped a hedge like a foxhound".

Up to 1936, the several families who hired rowing boats in Bowness Bay were in fierce opposition; then an Association was formed and, sensibly, the boatmen worked together. In the

I HAVE CHATTED with men who remembered when the promenade at Bowness Bay was of wood. Planking stretched between the shingly shore and the roadway. Trees grew tall and heavy-limbed beyond the high wall which marked the limit of the Belsfield grounds. The planks of the promenade had gaps between them and Bowness lads knew where they could gain access to the gloomy region. Here they looked for lost coins. Sand dredged from the lake was landed at Bowness Bay, to be riddled beside the pier.

Boating has been a feature of the Bay for well over a century. For years, the boatmen with rowing boats for hire were hoarse with shouting not only at passers-by but above the sounds made by their rivals. Until the early 1930s, each family worked for itself and competition was intense. Then, sensibly, the boatmen banded together, pooling resources and profits, though each man continued to be responsible for his own craft. The Windermere-type rowing boat is a local product, with larch planking three-eighths of an inch thick and with mahogany seats.

Tebay, Hodgson, Bispham, Fleming, Campbell and other Bowness families kept boating alive. The boats in our picture had been used on the lake for over 60 years, a tribute to the care in maintenance, though in 1960 one of the boatmen lamented to me that boats that were being hired by visitors were not being treated as well as they had been.

Dare I hope that at least one of the old type of rowing boat has been preserved?

early 1950s, when I chatted with Bert Hodgson, 230 rowing boats and some 36 motor boats operated from the Bay. The season extended from Easter to the end of September. Bert had become a little concerned even then at acts of vandalism. "Some people pay 3s a hire to take a boat on the lake and they think they have bought it". He watched as two boats were being deliberately rammed by people who gave whoops of delight as the craft collided.

The old Bowness Bay was a centre for tradition and high craftsmanship in boat-building. Tom Storey, who died in 1953, was building boats at 96. At the workshops of Messrs. Borwick I met Bill Bland, who started building boats in 1899. This was not long after Isaac Borwick had started the firm, in partnership with Nathaniel Shepherd. That partnership was dissolved in 1900. Each man went on to make a name for himself in the annals of Lakeland boat-building.

Borwicks built Windermere-type yachts, motor launches, racing hydroplanes capable of speeds up to 80 miles an hour, and rowing boats. Hydroplanes were under construction from 1920. Each craft was like a giant wooden shoe, but perfectly streamlined and adapted for skimming the water under power. A popular model, the two-pointer, touched the water in two places, each merely the size of a hand. During the 1939-45 war, lifeboats were made for the Merchant Navy and over 30 seaplane tenders were produced for the RAF.

Nathaniel Shepherd had five sons. They all followed him into the business, building many fine Windermere yachts, to a design by P.C. Crossley. The Windermere craft, which is 17 feet long at the waterline, was regarded as the fastest in the world for its size. "Although they may look alike, no two are precisely the same", said Wilfred Shepherd. "The weight of lead on the keel differs with each craft. The governing factor is the length at the waterline. The wood used is chiefly mahogany, the best obtainable". In 1907, when the firm employed about 30 men, they made 20 centreboard sailing boats for export to Spain and the year 1938 saw the construction of a 56ft passenger-carrying launch, the *Princess Margaret Rose,* which eventually was being used on Derwentwater.

At Borwicks, Bill Bland and I chatted in a room heady with the smell of varnish and new wood. The floor was littered with shavings. Men and apprentices were busy at benches on the beginnings of yet another large craft. Bill had served his apprenticeship with Tom Hayton, whose workshops were demolished when the promenade was built about 1912. It was all handwork. "I've sawn as many as 12 pairs of oars out of 2½ inch planks – using a hand saw. It would take me over an hour to cut out one pair". Work at the shop began at 7 a.m. and ended at 5.30 p.m., with half an hour for lunch. "Ten hours a day – with five on Saturdays!"

Craft up to 50 feet long were created at Borwicks. Early in the century, an electrically-driven boat was produced for the *Lodore Hotel,* for service on Derwentwater. "Two electric boats were owned by the hotel. While one was operating on the lake, the other was having its batteries re-charged. Power came from a dynamo operated by water from Lodore Falls". From 1934 until 1949, Borwicks were building over 90 craft a year. Bill Bland estimated that he had a hand in constructing well over 400 boats. I met Bill's son, Bruce, who told me that rowlocks used on Borwick boats were offset, a design invented by the late Tom Hayton. It was never patented. Borwicks gave the work of making rowlocks to a blacksmith.

In a tribute to the boat-builders of Bowness Bay, Miss Barbara Hall wrote: "Local building has a perfection and finish seldom seen elsewhere. For a long time almost all the Club boats have been built at the edge of the lake, and generations of craftsmen have built little ships whose smallest detail is a delight to the eye. Varnished decks, mahogany hulls, often varnished but sometimes painted, polished brass or chromium glinting in the sun, give the racing fleet their ultimate touch of trim and spotless efficiency".

The first steamers on Windermere, in 1859, were *Lord of the Isles* (destroyed by fire) and *Lady of the Lake*. When a rival company appeared, and to retain customer loyalty, these steamers carried passengers round the lake free of charge. Each passenger was given a glass of beer. Walter Beggs served for 43 years on their successors, the "railway steamers". Some of them went as far as the *Swan Hotel* boathouse at Newby Bridge. "These were two-bowed boats, with a rudder at each end. One of them had paddles. You see, there was no turning round in the river. All they needed to do was to reverse engines and use the other rudder!"

For many years, coal was used to power the "railway boats" on Windermere. Each night, at Lakeside, before the crew dispersed, the coal stocks on board were replenished. A single vessel needed at least 30 swills of coal, each swill (large basket) holding a hundredweight. In dry weather, coal dust blew everywhere and it was then necessary to wash the boat down. William McGarr was serving on the Windermere steamer *Swift* in 1930 when, between Bowness and Waterhead, someone pointed out the sleek form of *Miss England,* the racing craft in which Sir Henry Segrave intended to make some record bids. The boat was under tow to the area of the measured mile. *Swift,* having visited Lakeside, started on the return voyage. In the time taken to call at and depart from the jetty, *Miss England,* having begun her first run, was wrecked at speed, through hitting a floating log. Sir Henry was dead.

LAKESIDE, AT THE FOOT OF WINDERMERE.

TYING UP THE "TEAL" AT BOWNESS PIER.

Occasionally, I was allowed to stand on the bridge of a lake steamer, having a clear all-round view of the low wooded hills around Windermere. Mansions not properly seen by road-users were seen in well-tended grounds. The captain's eyes did not stray from the lake. As Storrs approached, he looked for the shallows which are well buoyed. The most notorious underwater hazard is known as Oven Bottom. In the mid-1960s, I heard from the crew of a boat about such unusual sights on Windermere as a helicopter and a caravan on floats, driven by outboard engines, an ingenious craft which was later barred from the lake. The owner of Belle Island caused a ripple of interest when he began to commute between the island and the mainland in an amphibious motor car.

It was at the approach to Bowness Bay that the greatest concentration was needed by the captain and helmsman. Racing yachts were moored just outside the bay. Rowing boats and self-drive hire motor boats scurried about like varnished water beetles. The direction of the wind was studied and a decision reached as to which side of the pier would be used. The steamer nudged the pier and was tied up. Soon we were cruising again. The engines operated "half astern". Ropes from the stern guided the vessel around the pier end so that she was facing towards the open water. It was a routine known as "back spring". Below deck, I sampled some of the caterer's ham sandwiches and stood up now and again to watch through a porthole the slow passing of the wooded, sunlit shore.

The scientists at Ferry House, headquarters of the Freshwater Biological Association, told me about their researches into Windermere's diverse life. I heard of the first serious work on the Cumbrian lakes, which was begun prior to the 1914-18 war by W.H. Pearsall, FRS, later Professor of Botany at University College, London. All his visits to the lakes were made from his home at Dalton-in-Furness using a bicycle. He took samples from the various lakes and carried them home in bottles, which he packed into his rucksack. It was Professor Pearsall who pointed out that presumably after the Ice Age all the lakes were in much the same condition but had been changing ever since, some having changed more rapidly than others. One of the factors that speeds up this change considerably is human settlement and the disposal of sewage into the lakes.

The Association started in a way that was typically English – as a purely private enterprise. In the late 1920s, a number of University professors and those interested in waterworks and fishing detected a need for a research institute of a type that had existed on the Continent before the turn of the century. They looked for funds. The institute came into being in 1931 when £500 had been subscribed and the first home was Wray Castle, that imposing but sham building on the north-western shore of the lake, which was rented from the National Trust. The research body shared the premises with the Youth Hostels' Association. The FBA was awarded a governmental grant that increased as the years went by. By moving to Ferry House (the former *Ferry Hotel*, built in 1879), the research staff had more space – and some glorious views of Windermere.

Dr. Winifred Frost told me about the char, *Salvelinus alpinus,* which is present in a number of our lakes. A typical Lakeland char is from 10 to 12 inches long, and the breeding male is notable because his belly assumes a brilliant orange-red colour and white edges to the fins have an enamel-like intensity. The breeding female has a "spawning dress" that is less bright than the male's attire. Both have olive-green backs. Dr. Frost told me that the char is a member of the salmon family. Its distribution is circumpolar. In some countries – Russia, Norway and Canada among them – the fish is migratory, hatching in fresh water and eventually migrating to the sea to feed. The char then returns to the water of its birth. In Britain, the char is landlocked. It is

Afloat on Windermere. Above – Just discernible near Ferry Hotel is the old rowing boat used as a ferry. Below, left – One of the craft from the Bowness Steamboat Museum. Below, right – "Teal", on a regular holidaytime voyage from Lakeside to Waterhead.

presumed that this happened at the end of the Ice Age, which in Lakeland would be about 14,000 years ago. The char is now found in Haweswater, Crummock Water, Buttermere, Ennerdale Water, Coniston Water and Windermere, where it frequents the cold depths, up to 100ft and more from the surface dazzle.

If you were to go into a Lakeland tackle shop and ask for some equipment for catching char, the owner would give you a pitying look. Over two million Britons regularly enjoy angling, but maybe only 30 are familiar with the char-fishing technique. Of these 30, there may be a dozen "hardened cases", as one of the enthusiasts described them to me. We had been chatting by Bowness Bay. Dr. Frost's research indicated that Windermere has two different populations of char; they are made distinctive by their breeding habits, one population spawning in November, in quite shallow water, from six to 15 ft deep, and the other population spawning from mid-February to mid-March in deep water, from 50 to 60 ft.

The char, a worthy quarry, is trolled for from a boat. It was Norman Smith and W.G. Bewsher, of Bowness, who first explained the technique to me; they listed the successful char-fisherman's requirements. The boat should be strong enough to withstand wind and weather. The rod, for which a special rest is screwed on to the side of the boat, has a length of 15 feet, being traditionally made of ash, though Norman Smith showed me a rod made of bamboo. Two rods are employed; they extend from the boat at an angle of 45 degrees, looking for all the world like primitive wings.

The main fishing line has a length of 90 feet. Char-fishermen are individualistic, and a variety of methods are used for securing line to rod. A bell is attached to the end of the rod to warn the angler of a bite. He rejoices when the pliant rod shakes and the bell rings. He is even more pleased if the tip of the rod goes under water! In the old days, lines were treated with a mixture of linseed oil and varnish for durability. Modern materials are more durable. The 90 ft of line is kept taut by a lead weight called a "ploomb"; it has a tail which prevents it from spinning incessantly and twisting the tackle.

Picture, then, a boat on Windermere, with a long line extending downwards to a weight. Now imagine lines going off horizontally, spaced at 10 to 12 ft. These are the tail lines, of some 20lb breaking strain, to which the bait is attached. Years ago, live minnows were used in trolling for char. From about the 1820s, the spinner became the lure most in favour. To a spinner is attached a treble hook. The spinner is fashioned of metal – of bronze, brass, copper, even gold and silver, taken from old watches. A combination of two metals may be employed, as for example the laying of a strip of silver on bronze or a diagonal strip of silver on brass. Spinners turn because the metal at the tail has been bent. An exception is the spinner on the highest line, which turns from the head. Once the boat is moving, with the lines in place, it must not stop or some terrible tangles develop!

The fishing season extends from March 3 to September 30, but April and May were regarded by my two informants as the best months for the sport. Evidence from the lines suggests that the char are then nearer to the surface; at the end of summer into autumn they are usually in the cold depths. A char-fisherman has no fixed hours for the sport. Norman Smith told me he liked fishing in the early morning, from about 7 a.m. It was then very quiet on the lake. The man who taught Mr. Bewsher how to fish for char had an ambition, which he never realised, to fish by moonlight. In 1976, a man was on the lake all day and then he fished through the night. He caught 41 char.

Both men agreed that, at the end of the day, eating freshly-caught char is a delectable

OLD AND NOT-SO-OLD CRAFT ON WINDERMERE.

experience. Said Mr. Bewsher: "If anyone wants more than a three-quarter pound char, which has been served with all the trimmings, then he's a glutton!"

Miss M. McCormack's prime interest was in perch. She prefaced her remarks by saying that at Millerground, near where the Wynlass Beck enters Windermere, is a prime area for perch angling in autumn. It has also been a study area for scientists connected with the FBA. I was in the Association's boat, at the approach to Millerground, when an echo sounder was switched on; it probed through 30 feet of water to the bed of the lake, recording what appeared to be a huge black umbrella. This was a shoal of perch, the fish being packed into an area no more than 20 or 30 yards square.

On the bed of the lake, those fish were swimming on an underwater hill composed of rounded stones. Alert, vigorous fish, they flaunted their olive-green bodies (which are darkly marked by four or five bars) and their orange-red fins. Stout spines protruded from deep, well-fleshed bodies. Throughout the autumn they had fed well in Millerground area. Now they were full of fat, which would fortify them in winter, when they would be swimming, rather lethargically, in about 60 feet of water. Our knowledge of the life style of the Windermere perch has been painstakingly amassed by the FBA over many years.

The Association's interest began at Wray Castle, where in 1940 its director, Dr. E.B. Worthington, began experiments including the numerical reduction of perch and pike through trapping and netting. From 1942 until 1960, the perch investigations were the special responsibility of Mr. E.D. LeCren; Miss M. McCormack had been concerned with them from 1953. I met her in 1965. She told me that the purpose behind examining Millerground samples was to keep an eye on the weight of the perch. In 1939, this was 2oz and now the average was about 6oz, an increase brought about by the Windermere Perch Trap Fishery, which was operated in the North Basin of the lake from 1940 until 1949 and in the South Basin from 1941 to 1964. It was never intended to be an economic fishery, but during the war the British Fish Canners, of Leeds, took fish caught in Windermere and marked them under the name "Perchines". Two tins remained at Ferry House until recently. Then one tin exploded in a cupboard!

Large wire cages were being placed in the lake at the perch "beats" about a week before the spawning season began. These traps were unbaited, but perch entered them in such numbers that in the early days a hundredweight of fish was recovered from one trap and another trap collapsed under the weight of fish as it was being removed from the lake. (Each spawning season, the scientists also removed from the traps well over 80 eels, that varied in weight from ¼lb to 5lb). Miss McCormack mentioned the fairly steady harvest of pike – a hundred a year. Any pike caught in perch traps were marked with a metal loop tag on the jaw and returned to the lake alive. It was found that toads were spawning in some of the perch traps at a depth of 18ft., a fact never before recorded. One trap contained 350 toads, which normally are found spawning in shallow ponds.

Windermere is a much-used lake. A thousand craft a day furrow its surface at the height of the tourist season. Rights of way are generally thought of in relation to the land. Yet there is a right of way for any person to navigate a boat across the entire surface of Windermere. The bed of England's largest lake is owned by the South Lakeland District Council, who maintain a warden service on the boat. In summer, the National Park authority augments this service with a waterborne Ranger. The 1987-88 Report of the National Park authority states that this freedom is a great asset to the sailor, canoeist or owner of a cabin cruiser who wishes merely to

KESWICK IS FORTUNATE in being positioned near two of the most attractive lakes, Derwentwater and Bassenthwaite, and in having a building of the quality of the Moot Hall in a central position. The Moot Hall clock has a single hand. Keswick is a case of a town developed to serve local industry which has in recent times become a tourist centre and in effect the Northern Capital of the Lake District.

In early times, Keswick tradesmen had in mind the miners who went to ground at points in the fells. They recovered copper, lead and silver. Pencil-making was established, based originally on the Borrowdale plumbago. The pencil industry continues. The early tourists were fascinated by tales of the discovery and exploitation of the plumbago, also known as "black-lead". In the end, tourism triumphed. Keswick was first regarded as a resort for the better-off; the large hotels accommodated the gentry and nobility.

The magnificent Keswick Hotel, near the station, was opened in 1869, the railway having brought lots of visitors. Now the middle-class was important because of the numerical strength and affluence, but the railway company appears to have been keen to develop the goods traffic as well. Keswick's tourist growth was slow.

The heavy motor traffic, which once gave the Council much concern, now flows along a by-pass, the main problem at Keswick being one of parking. The road from the motorway at Penrith to West Cumbria crosses the exquisite Greta gorge on a concrete bridge, a conspicuous intrusion in a once attractive area.

potter about the lake at low speed. It becomes a problem, however, at busy times when it would be useful to be able to separate the high speed activities, water-ski-ing and power boating, from the more tranquil pursuits. "To some extent this zoning can be achieved through the use of speed limits which are imposed in the busier parts of the lake, but elsewhere there is nothing to stop a power boat from driving through the middle of a party of canoeists or to prevent a water skier from straying into an area used by swimmers!" The National Park authority carries out lake patrols on Coniston and Ullswater, where speed limits cover the entire lake surface and where levels of activity are much lower than on Windermere.

Windermere overflows as the river Leven. Just below Newby Bridge, on the Leven, Mr. H. Leck used to trap eels and send them – alive alive-o – to the market at Manchester. When the mill he owned was not operating he opened a sluice and water poured down an alternative bed to the river. In August and September, and at night, the water carried migratory eels along with it. They were stopped by a wooden grid and carried forward in a smaller amount of water to enter a box that was about five feet long, two feet wide and two feet high. Eels were transferred from here to a larger box that had been sunk in the ground nearby. When sufficient eels had been captured, they were consigned to Manchester by rail.

Mr. Leck took over from John and William Knowles. There was a spectacular catch of eels in their day. Only a few eels were stirring because of a drought. Then, about 10 p.m., during the first week of October, 1921, after rain had been falling for several hours, the men went to inspect the trap. It was full of eels. The sluice gate was temporarily closed to stop more eels entering. Lanterns were called for. The men worked all night. "Over 30 hundredweights of eels were placed in the keep ..." When the three year-old elvers are running upstream to Windermere in the spring, they had no trouble surmounting the weir, for there was a fish ladder to help them.

Keswick presides over two major lakes – Derwentwater and Bassenthwaite Lake. I enjoyed boatsmen's tales, heard at the Landing near Friars Crag. The Keswick and Derwentwater Launch Company was formed in 1933, ending a period of cut-throat competition among families with pleasure craft for hire. Herbert Birkett remarked to me that "men wanting trade used to walk up as far as the pavilion in Station Road to meet passengers coming off the trains ... The local council chased the proprietors back down to Peter's Field and would not allow them to go beyond that point. Eventually, the men had to remain at the stages". Competition was tough. "The men used to get into two's and three's and throw a coin in the air. The winner was given the chance of approaching the next party of visitors. The charge before the Great War was 1s an hour per person, with price reductions for groups".

The steamer *Lorna Doone,* which plied for hire on Derwentwater, was a "herring boat" converted to take about 50 passengers. It was owned by Joseph Hodgson, who then sold it to some men from Whitehaven. They collected it from the isthmus on which it had been beached, floating off the *Lorna Doone* without remembering to close the sea cocks. The boat sank. Barrels were assembled to give the necessary buoyancy for raising the boat and taking her across the bay. Here a large tractor hauled the boat on to the shore. The men now made their second major mistake, forgetting to drain the water from the boat; part of the bottom was torn out. The remains of the *Lorna Doone* were set on fire. Another old steamer, the *Derwent,* which could carry 23 passengers, was converted to a petrol engine and ran for a few years before being scrapped. Coal for the steamers was stored in a cabin on the shore. When petrol engines were introduced, the boat proprietors collected "Crown Spirit" from a store at the railway station. It cost 10d a gallon. A regular purchaser received a rebate at the end of the season if he had used a large amount.

When Norman Harrop was the boatman on Bassenthwaite Lake, we discussed angling, especially for pike, and I heard that in 1957 Pat Corie landed a 31½lb fish. A visiting angler who hooked a 5½lb pike was startled as he drew it into the boat, for the captive fish was snatched by a much bigger pike, which took it for about 200 yards and then released it. Bassenthwaite, I gathered, is a warm weather lake. "The fish tend to bite better when it's warm. The best sport is from July to early September, when the weed beds are in full growth". Pike are less evident in winter – and then there is some difficulty for an angler in finding perch as live bait; it tends to go into the deeper water. In the early 1970s, perch were common, a good fish averaging about 5oz, though Norman Harrap watched a perch make the scales dip at 3lb 4oz. It was caught at Beck Foot by his uncle, Frank, who was using worm. "Get among a shoal of perch, and the line doesn't get really wet; you're constantly pulling out fish. One man arrived back at the moorings with over 1½ cwt of fish!" The lake has a run of sea trout and salmon. The scarcest – though in many ways, the most interesting fish – is the vendace, a denizen of the deeps. Success with vendace comes to the angler who goes out specifically for this species and has the right tackle.

In its Silurian setting, Coniston Water has affinities with Windermere. Around its head are the great hills of the Coniston range. The "Thorstanes Watter" of Norman times is nearly six miles long, lying wide open to the sunshine and vulnerable to southerly gales, which soon turn it choppy. In the west, the hills do not spring directly from the water's edge. In the east, the Furness Fells, now covered with dark, drool conifers, rise with moderate steepness from the exposed rocks at the lake shore and have caused the narrow road to take a switchback course. Coniston Old Man and his craggy attendants are mirrored in the lake on tranquil days.

The lake is best seen, in its splendidly varied setting, from the deck of the *Gondola*. Only two islands break the expanse of water. These are Peel Island and Fir Island. Gales in the autumn of 1846 wrecked a third island, one of the floating variety, which in its prime was 20 yards square and finely covered with birches. A contemporary report stated: "It got stranded among the reeds at Nibthwaite during a high wind and heavy flood, and has never been able to get off again".

W.G. Collingwood, writer and artist, remembered Peel Island for its "pretty little cove for harbour, and a well-blackened fire-spot where many a picnic kettle has boiled". Formerly known as Montague Island, after the lords of the manor, it was "Wild Cat Island" to Arthur Ransome, author of the Lakeland stories of adventure. The nearby Fir Island changes its status according to the water level. At "low water" it is merely a promontory, easily reached on foot. The dominant pines are a favourite roosting place for cormorants. This fact would have appealed to Ransome.

Coniston Water has two basins. One of them is up to 180ft deep. Within the subterranean valley lie the remains of Donald Campbell's speedboat *Bluebird,* which sank during a water speed record bid in 1967. The body of a brave man was never recovered. Elsewhere, the depth varies from about 30ft to 50ft. Shallows are uncommon. Captain Hammill, veteran skipper of *Gondola,* used to say: "There are few places on Coniston Lake where I could not put the prow into green fields while the stern was over deep water". I saw a model of the *Gondola* in the museum at Coniston – a model made by Captain Hamill, who served on this steamer for nearly 50 years. The museum also had a photograph of him, with the model he had constructed. He was a tidy-looking man, with a dense white beard. In 1976, no one would have envisaged that the *Gondola* would sail again. I observed what remained of her when I leaned on some roadside

IN THE PICTURE is the head of Ullswater with a mirror-image of the flanking fells that normally appear to leap from the water, as the mountains leap directly from the fjords in Norway. The M6 made Ullswater easily accessible to a vast number of people; they approach from the right direction, the landscape becoming grander with every mile.

Several times a day, Ullswater reflects two yacht-like, green-hulled boats, former steamers, that ply between Glenridding and Pooley Bridge. Each boat has a black and white funnel adorned with the head of a stag. Jack Kirkpatrick, who had a long working life as an engineer before his retirement, assisted in the conversion from steam to diesel in 1933. He told me that in the days of steam, the coke needed as fuel arrived from the North East at Penrith station and was transported to Pooley Bridge by a man called Lancaster, the proud owner of a horse and cart.

For many years, the steamers of Ullswater were the main form of transport for heavy goods, such as slate, coal and groceries. Jack Kirkpatrick recalled for me when visitors on train excursions from Bradford and Leeds disembarked at Langwathby and were taken by wagonettes to Pooley Bridge, the people being separated into "first" and "second" class passengers. Lord Lonsdale was "king of the castle". It was at his insistence that a change was made to the afterdeck of the "Raven", a line being painted around it in yellow, which was Lordy's favourite colour.

The lake steamers were indispensable until 1929, when the Ribble Bus Company began to operate in the area. In the 1930s, with improving roads and more reliable transport, the steamers were being regarded locally as quaint survivals from the old days. That was before the upsurge in tourist interest. Today, the graceful boats convey thousands of appreciative passengers up and down Ullswater, which is our second largest lake.

railings near Nibthwaite and looked towards the lake. The boat was partly submerged and in a sad condition. The owner, Mr. A.J. Hatton, who bought her in 1966, had done his best to preserve Lakeland's oldest steam yacht, but his efforts had several times been delayed by vandals, one of whom actually used dynamite. He had a quiet confidence in the fact that *Gondola* would one day be restored. She became the property of The National Trust, who carefully raised and floated her to the head of the lake, where she was taken out and the iron hull was sent to Barrow for attention. *Gondola* was lovingly restored. On the day she was re-commissioned, she was immaculate.

The *Gondola,* an elegant steam yacht, 85ft long, with a beam of 14ft, operated between Waterhead pier at Coniston and the jetty at Lake Bank. Originally owned by the local Railway Company, who wished to extend the tourist facilities in the district, she was made of Low Moor iron by Jones and Quiggan at Liverpool. *Gondola* was launched in 1859, the year in which the line itself had been opened. I heard that the original design incorporated a horizontal funnel, at the stern. On the day she was launched, she entered the water with a full head of steam, but water flowed up the funnel and put out the boiler fire! Originally, steam was supplied from a Furness Railway-type locomotive boiler, using coke, an experimental arrangement that was afterwards modified to burn coal. The arrangement of the cabin was unique. The ribs of the hull continued upwards between the windows and curved over in the form of complete iron hoops to support the cabin roof. *Gondola* served the lake users for some 80 years. In 1908, *The Lady of the Lake* was constructed to replace her, and yet both craft were operated. It was to be the *Lady* who was scrapped, in 1950.

Until about 1920, Buttermere, Crummock Water and Loweswater were regularly netted for fish, which were sold to local hotels. In the period between being caught and disposed of, the fish were kept alive in wooden boxes set in running water. Kendal Vickers, born at Loweswater in 1893, used to tell me about the netting, with which he had assisted. The net was about 100 yards long, a yard deep at the ends and some 30 yards in the middle; the net was weighed down by lead and the top was kept buoyant by a string of corks. One end of the net was fastened to the shore and the other managed from a boat. "We had tremendous catches of fish – salmon, sea trout and brown trout". Char were lifted from Buttermere and Crummock Water. This species lived in the deep water and had to be sought with weighted line and spinners. Potted char was considered a delicacy. Mr. Vickers preferred his fish – fried!

Wastwater has the grandest setting. I have seen it through a rent in clouds en route from Wasdale Head to Steeple. I have *not* seen it from the ridge above the Screes, for each time I go this way – from Eskdale back to Eskdale, via the Screes and Miterdale – the Weather Clerk draws a curtain of cloud across the sun and then lags the earth with mist. My best views have come from Great Gable, four miles to the north of the lake, and from the lakeside road that pays homage to the topography, having a winding, up and down course, but at one point offering a view of lake and clustering mountains that is so sublime the National Park chose the outline of it as an emblem.

Wasdale is the lake in which part of an electric cable was sunk so that it would not be conspicuous. Electrical power came to Wasdale Head as recently as 1977. Over 20 years ago, ideas were put forward that would not create a blemish on this outstanding landscape. Some schemes were turned down on the grounds of cost. Then NORWEB and The National Trust reached a solution – and financial support came from the Countryside Commission, with free labour under the Job Creation programme. The scheme involved two short lengths of 11,000

The grace of steam-powered craft. Above – "Gondola", the former railway steamer which still steams, under the auspices of The National Trust. For many years, the battered hull of this famous boat lay on the bed of the lake near Nibthwaite. Right – Part of the large collection at the Bowness Steamboat Museum.

FROM NEAR the head of Haweswater, a visitor looks at the islands of this reservoir – islands which, in the picture, show the tidemarks betokening a drought – to wild little Riggindale, beyond which looms High Street. Little of human consequence appears to have happened in Riggindale, and with a length of about one-and-a-half miles it is more of a recess than a dale. At its head are formidable crags, with some corries. At the other end, Riggindale has an abrupt ending on the shore of Haweswater. The southern side of Riggindale is craggy, with rowan and birch. To the north, an upsweeping fellside does not seem to have recovered from the shock of being over-run and scoured by glacial ice. Here are screes and coarse grasses.

It is not easy to explain the appeal of the dale to anyone who lacks an interest in natural history and who would be unmoved by hearing a raven's croak or seeing the delicate pink flowers of bird's-eye primrose. Fell ponies give to this wild, austere little dale an Icelandic flavour. Now and again, a golden eagle crosses the dale or, high soaring, appears as little more than a speck against a cloud.

Outside the rut, hinds and young stags from Martindale find their way into Riggindale as springtime greens up the land by the beck. The sheep, Herdwicks and Swaledales, by their incessant grazing, keep the ground vegetation short and trim.

The aria of a ring ouzel on the crags is heard above the babble of voices from the Canada geese squabbling on the nearby reservoir …

volt overhead lines and the laying of about five miles of cable, half of it underground and the rest along the bed of Wastwater. Stanley Bulmer, NORWEB's Lakeland area manager, said that although the Board had a number of submarine cables in service, several years had elapsed since the last was laid. His engineers regarded the Wasdale submarine cable as "an interesting challenge".

Manchester converted Thirlmere into a reservoir under a scheme that received Parliamentary approval in 1879. Sensitive souls like Canon Rawnsley, John Ruskin and the Bishop of Carlisle were appalled at the consequences, especially as a new road was blasted along the eastern side, high above the lake level. (Yet when the reservoir was officially opened in 1894, Canon Rawnsley was asked to lead the assembled dignatories in prayer, which he did – at length). A further shock, in 1908, was the wholesale planting of conifers, almost 2,000 acres of conifers, swamping the lower fellsides where nature intended a much lighter array of deciduous trees to grow. Thirlmere's water was found to be so pure it could be delivered directly to the taps of the city, over 90 miles away. A purification plant was considered unnecessary. The upshot was the Manchester prohibited access to the immediate area by the public in the cause of a clean water supply. (Not until 1982, when a treatment works was constructed, would it be possible to allow the public a degree of access to Thirlmere and the land immediately around it).

Manchester now sought a greater share in the rainfall of the Lake District. A private bill promoted in 1919 led, after many years, to the creation of the Haweswater reservoir (1939) with attendant work in Wet Sleddale (1966). Water goes via Longsleddale to a junction with the Thirlmere pipeline. In 1988, the government's plans to privatise water undertakings were made known, leading to another flurry of activity on the part of conservationists. The future of the big reservoirs is uncertain.

For Haweswater, Manchester Corporation set a concrete dam in the mouth of old Mardale, extending a pleasant mere into a reservoir that laps against the feet of a horse-shoe of fells at the dalehead. The Corporation also constructed a hotel; it is the only inhabited building throughout the length of the main dale. The quite large hotel stands on a ledge beside the road, 120 feet above the chilly water of the reservoir. The hotel has its back against a fellside covered with a mixture of indigenous tree species. The wood is the haunt of red squirrels, also of deer. Buzzards mew as they circle on the thermals. Deer may be seen on open ground across the water. When I attended a meeting of the north-west branch of the British Deer Society, we sat in a shady lounge, listening to our guest speaker but mindful of the fellside, which was in full sunshine, with half a dozen red hinds grazing between the patches of bleached bracken fronds!

On a visit to the district by the Ullswater pack, the hounds pursued a fox through the back garden of the hotel. Supporters of the pack then gathered in the building to give a lusty rendering of the local hunting ditty. "The Mardale Hunt". Anglers know the reservoir for its lively brown trout and the char that inhabit the depths for most of the year, when they are beyond the reach of anglers' tackle.

It is the diversity of lakes that impresses the visitor. Windermere, in the Silurian countryside, where the hills are neither high nor sharp, is over 10 miles long, with promontories and reedy bays attractive to wintering waterfowl – to goldeneye and tufted duck in particular. The Windermere mallard/Aylesbury ducks carry out commando raids on picnicing parties. Some pairs nest on moored craft. At the peak of the season, the lake might have 1,000 assorted craft upon it. Ullswater is the second largest lake; my favourite laybye is at Gowbarrow, not too far from where clumps of daffodils exerted an appeal to the Wordsworths. Roosting gulls by the thousand descend on Ullswater in winter, when they are not likely to be disturbed by visitors.

The lake edges, like the high ridges, bear the weight of the human foot which, in some parts of Lakeland, have destroyed a former rich habitat and created a gravel beach, which is a botanical desert.

Crummock Water, Buttermere and Loweswater, in a quiet western dale, provide good examples of communities of plants and animals associated with lakes having low nutrient levels. Ennerdale Water is the only major lake without a public road along its length. Not only is the lake unnatural in its shoreline, having been dammed to provide water for coastal settlements, but the dale is clogged with conifers that, happily, will have their grim corporate appearance modified by landscaping in years to come.

Esthwaite Water is a special favourite of mine. Here is a substantial reed-bed, with attendant reed warblers, at the northern part of their breeding range, and a pair of great-crested grebe which tether their soggy nest to the vegetation. I park my car in a well-shielded park and eagerly scan the lake for wintering wildfowl. Once, several mute swans were drifting just offshore, waiting for some tit bits of food, when the long, dark, shiny form of a cormorant surfaced between them, to their great surprise.

Whooper swans that nested by the lakes and in the wild river valleys of Iceland fly 500 miles to Scotland, some to venture southwards to Lakeland. I see them on Grasmere. Elterwater suits them, for the name is said to mean "swan lake". I have watched greylags by Derwentwater and at the small but very popular Tarn Hows (the Tarns) above Coniston and Hawkshead. Bassenthwaite, with its reedy bays, is a prime wintering ground for wild duck.

The National Park Plan acknowledges the diversity of lakes and tarns. "In addition to the larger and better known lakes, there are numerous other small lakes and tarns in the Lake District. Some are tucked away in the valleys in spots not frequently visited, others are peppered over the higher ground. A number have specific nature conservation interests. The more productive may support small fisheries. But perhaps the greatest value of these small areas of water is their contribution to the diversity of scenery and to the basic character of the National Park … The NPA's policies will give full recognition to the diverse qualities of the lakes … and take account of the amount of recreational development and access which already exists".

WHOOPER SWANS, WINTER VISITORS TO LAKELAND.

LIFE IN THE DALES

SIDNEY COLE, who for many years resided at Brownrigg, Caldbeck, "back o' Skiddaw", was aware of having lived through a bloodless revolution in Lakeland – the transition from hand work, performed by a host of people, to the use of sophisticated machines, operated by a few. Sidney had ploughed with a wheel-less swing plough. He remembered when Andrew Scott mowed a three and a-half acre field with a scythe. When Sidney arrived in Caldbeck, there was only one binding machine, belonging to Chris Hewetson. Everyone else harvested with an ordinary repeater. The sheaves were hand-tied. Many people were poor and did not realise it, because so many others shared in the austerity. A man bought a new suit every five or even 10 years. People clattered about in clogs.

Sidney Cole had built up a huge collection of bygones, domestic and industrial. His interest was in ordinary objects, not scarce and potentially valuable antiques. I saw many of these curios at Knocker, his home on the fellside – a habitation made from two cottages, one of which had held the knocker-up. "In old days, about 1,100 people lived in Caldbeck, which had woollen and bobbin mills, even a brewery. Remember too, there were some productive mines up Roughton Gill and that some of the workers set off to walk to work at between 5 a.m. and 7 a.m." The rap of the knocker-up's cane against a bedroom window, more usually thought of as a custom of the Lancashire mill towns, roused a workaday Cumberland community.

Chris Hewetson helped Sidney Cole to become established at Brownrigg, a farm standing on the 1,000 ft contour. The choice of farm was excellent, the land being of very good loam on limestone. In 1919, the farm was primitive. Dora, his wife, told me that the only source of water was a well at the back of the house "and the heavens above". The illumination was provided by a single-burner oil lamp. Said Sidney: "Brownrigg carried such a small quantity of stock that you were thought to be in a big way if you had 25 cows and six or eight calves. The same-sized farm today (1976) would carry from 60 to 80 cattle". In those distant days, income tax was gauged at double the rent, and anything a man made over that he kept. Rates were 1s. 11d in the £. "You didn't need to carry a lot of money. Neighbours helped each other, as with sheep-clipping and harvesting. If I had need of a binder, I'd borrow that belonging to Chris Hewetson; I could also borrow an extra horse to draw it".

Transport was cheap. A man might have a "spring cart" (a cross between a buggy and a big heavy cart) and surplus farm stock was walked to Wigton. "You'd take the horse and cart there once a fortnight for essential purchases. The cost of living was negligible. Why, I've often had my own oats ground at the mill. We all grew a certain amount of oats in those days. Now it's all barley. We'd not look at barley then ..." The farmer sold from his farm butter, eggs and wool. He would sell a cow when it came up to its third calf. He might also have a foal for disposal. "A pair of horses I bought lasted me 30 years before they were finished; they had scarcely cost me a halfpenny. When I came to Caldbeck, a complete set of new shoes for a horse cost only 8s. 8d".

With the rapid decline in the once great labour force, the countryside is now a relatively quiet place. At the time of the 1914-18 war, a lad would be hired for the half year at £6.50 (if he was a "big un") or £5 (for a "little 'un"). If a lad proved useless, he could be persuaded to leave by having his bed made up on the byre loft. The term "loft" became synonymous with bed. "A farm man would fetch a laal yawn and say: 'Weel, I'se had a good day, and I'se tired. I'se gaan on t'loft.'"

The dalesfolk perpetuated an ancient round of activity against a backdrop provided by some of the finest landscape in Britain. It was a farmer at Hartsop who observed: "There's gey little bottomland i' this part o' t'Lake District. That's t'trouble. Valleys are too narrow, and there's not mich flat in t'bottom. Flattest bit is covered by lake!"

Wasdale – to me, the most appealing of the dales – is generally thought of as wintry valley, which is not the case. The sea is not far away, the lake and the dale are at low elevation (in its deepest part, the bed of Wastwater is actually below sea level); when there is snow and ice on the fells the dale often experiences a moderating wind from the Irish Sea. Yet Wasdale has a reputation for climatic excesses. When I was there in 1980, no rain had fallen for six weeks and across the dalehead – Wordsworth's "fertile little plain" – lay a pattern of fine cracks where the earth was parting at the seams. It sometimes rains! The last time I walked along the ridge across the Screes, I saw scarcely anything for mist and driving rain. Wasdale Head's little church is served by the vicar of Gosforth. As recently as 1977, it had no dedication and so as part of the celebrations at the coming of electricity, a service was held and St. Olave became the church's patron, mainly because of the Norse associations with this area. Seventy-five people packed into a church which normally accommodates only 50.

Wasdale Head terminates a western valley in the cleanest, most majestic way. The bare bones of the landscape stick through the green skin of the earth and is there another dale with a finer headpiece? Great Gable, with its bold conical appearance, is everyone's idea of what a good mountain should look like. In immediate attendance are Kirk Fell, Yewbarrow and Lingmell. The dale ends with a flourish of trees – with oak, sycamore, larch, as well as some upstart conifers and the inevitable clusters of rhododendrons. One also remembers the profusion of stone – so much stone that it forms a futuristic pattern of stone walls and was piled up here and there in a desperate attempt to clear the land.

It was in the summer of 1956 that I first met Jim and Joss Naylor at Wasdale Head. The brothers were haymaking. Thick swathes were falling neatly behind a mowing machine. The Naylors had been pointed out to me as clever hunters of foxes, though they gave much of the credit to their three cur dogs and two fox terriers – especially the curs, Bell (then 15 years old) and her two seven-year-old daughters, Smart and Jip. In five years they had accounted for over 120 foxes. Sharp-featured with lithesome body and nimble mind, the fox is respected but not loved by the fell farmers. Up here in Wasdale, foxes average 10-12lb in weight, though one animal was "long in the leg and terribly big made". When caught, it weighed 20lb. Working together, often without human guidance, the dogs ran down foxes, and one fox was killed after only 100 yards.

Wasdale, which had many farms and quite a large population, was experiencing a social change with the amalgamation of small farms into large units. At The Gill, Nether Wasdale, I heard from 83 year old W.J. Gass that what is now one farm was once five small farms. He was in the hayfield, wielding a fork. He told me that he had lived at The Gill for 50 years and that when he sold his first batch of draft ewes on taking over the place he walked the sheep about eight miles, stood all day at the market and received the equivalent of 50p each for them. "That", he said with pride, "was my start".

Veterans told me about the days when most farm jobs were performed by hand – when, at the edge of human memory, men with straight-shafted scythes strode as a team across the meadows and laid the grass in broad swathes. The blades were sharpened by a device known as a "strickle", a piece of willow which, when not in use, was attached to the shaft and helped to give the implement balance. The strickle was pitted with holes, spread with bacon fat and dusted with a fine, hard sand collected from some upland tarns. The sand worked its way into the holes, was held by the fat and gave the strickle an abrasive face.

Dudley Hoys, writer of Lakeland short stories, lived at The Woolpack, Eskdale and, at the time I first met him, in the 1950s, was President of the Cumbrian Literary Group. Hoys had

Studies of Lakeland farmers. Above – *A two-dog man near Patterdale.* Left – *Spectators at the Herdwick pens, Eskdale Show, held at Boot.* Below – *At the head of Martindale. In the picture is the postbus from Penrith.*

been in the Army during the war. He decided to stay in Eskdale for a week or two while considering his future – and he stayed ever since! He was fond of talking about his adopted dale – about the river that rises at Esk Hause, between Esk Pike and Scafell, at 2,490 ft above sea level, and initially drops 1,000 ft in a mile.

Seathwaite Farm, at the head of Borrowdale, is generally recognised as the wettest inhabited spot in Lakeland. For as long as I can remember, it has been occupied by Edmondsons – three generations, each named Stanley – the descendants of John Edmondson who moved to this farm from Birkrigg in the Newlands Valley in 1916. The furniture was transported up Borrowdale in a huge van drawn by horses. (The National Trust became the owners of Seathwaite Farm in the 1940s).

The Seathwaite sheep graze some of the best-known fells in Lakeland – Glaramara, Esk Hause, Great End, Seathwaite Fell, the Gables, Base Brown and Brandreth. All lie within the parish boundary. In addition, the Edmondson sheep occupy land towards Black Sail, where they meet up with sheep from Wasdale and Buttermere. In the early 1970s, a helicopter was hired annually to lift to the fells about 30 tons of Rumevite, nourishing blocks, each weighing about 50lb. The blocks were to help the sheep meet the rigours of the Lakeland winter. "When we get to the end of January, the sheep are looking for them", said the second Stanley Edmondson, when we chatted in 1973.

In 1979, I reached Seathwaite Farm at the time of the last sheep dipping of the year. It was "tub time" for ewes which would occupy the local "heafs" the winter through. The Lakeland farmer dips his sheep against lice and scab. The routine was to mark the sheep, an indication of ownership; to dose any animals that might be afflicted by liver fluke and worms, and to totally immerse them in the "tub", which was in fact a concrete-sided trough, built within the old salve house.

To me, Seathwaite is the place where I can park a car near the fells – and a farm where light refreshments are sold. There is joy in drawing a cold drink up a straw into a parched mouth after hours spent trudging on the skyline under what can at times be a pitiless sun.

The Blands of Seatoller – like the Edmondsons of Seathwaite – have long been attached to their native "heaf". I recall a chat with Mrs. Noble Bland when most of the conversation was about the weather. I reached Seatoller just as a whirlwind developed in the new car park. Unexpectedly, on a hot and sunny day, wind plucked at a patch of dust, lifting it in a spiralling column to a height of about 20 ft. The whirlwind worked its way round the little park and left by the main gateway! The presence of dust rather than mud signified good weather, though some Lakeland folk would have taken the view that a whirlwind is a portend of rain in three days. The Blands were making hay using a new-fangled baler (this was the year 1970). In a chancy year, the men had been working till midnight and, with machine power, were continuing to gather the vital hay crop.

Kentmere and Longsleddale are like deep fingermarks on the fell country just north of Kendal. Neither has a through road, so an air of secrecy remains, yet walkers who plan to traverse the Kentmere Horseshoe must arrive early to claim car parking space near the old church. The dale is rarely out of sight to those who walk the airy ridges. When I last trudged that way, the felltops were in their winter white and a flock of snow buntings crossed an Arctic scene looking for the seed heads of moorland grasses.

A summer spectacle at Kentmere Hall before the 1914-18 war was the "boon clip", when the dalesfolk gathered at each farm in turn to rob the Herdwick sheep of their woolly jackets. At the Hall, about 40 creels (stools capable of holding shearer and sheep) were arranged in the yard.

"Everybody used to look forward to clipping day. You were fed, and at t'finish up there was a big sit-down in t'barn. Trestle tables and forms were set out. Wives and sarvant lasses were there to help. It was a real 'knife and fork' do, with a big roast and trimmings, apple tart with cream. You could drink either beer or tea". There followed a Clipping Party in an outbuilding. "I was never much of a dancer, but I used to enjoy listening to my old boss, Noble Gregg, as he played the melodeon. Dancing went on till well into t'morning".

Longsleddale seems to go on for ever. Travellers on the A6 north of Kendal see a road sign "Longsleddale 4½ miles". At this distance, they arrive at the dale church, having followed a winding, constricted road. Six miles from the main road are the farmsteads of Sadgill, where Norsefolk lived (the name Sadgill relating to a "saeter", or place of summer pasturage, by the gill). At eight miles from the A6, a traveller – now on foot – can look into Wren Gill, which is the source of the river Sprint. The flanking fells rise to the 2,000 ft. contour.

Farmhouses were well sited to cheat the worst of the weather. T.D. Walshaw, of Low Sadgill, told me how the wind tends to curl down the valley, so that when there is a howling gale a person might stand in the porch of his house in calm conditions. This valley is like a funnel. "You can sometimes stand and watch the clouds moving one way but detect the wind is moving in another direction!"

Low Sadgill, 620 ft above sea level, was constructed on rising ground, and consequently the back door is nine feet higher than the front door. Four generations of Fishwicks have lived at the nearby Sadgill Farm. The first, John, came from Howe End in Ennerdale and married an Airey, from Brockstone in Kentmere. Their son, Miles, who died in 1949, continued the family association, which at the time I first knew the area was being maintained by the grandsons, Tom and William Fishwick. On my most recent visit, I saw a great grandson hard at work. The "bottom land" totals 70 acres, but sheep from Sadgill venture to about 1,400 ft on Harter Fell and Goats Scar. "Herdwicks petered out but our sheep join up with Herdwicks kept in the Haweswater district", I was told by William. On such a stock farm, it is vital to keep up the endless drystone walls. "We have a terribly varied sort of stone on the walls – some good slate, bad slate, flinty stones and rounded ones that originally came from the beck".

Grisedale, one of the "little dales", is seen by walkers approaching Striding Edge on their way to Helvellyn. It was in Grisedale I heard of the life of the Lakeland shepherd from Harry Blamire, who for 33 years had farmed Braesteads, the last farm in the valley. He was the shepherd for the owner, Mr. Peter Scott, and was assisted by Denis, his son. Their charges were over 1,400 ewes and hoggs (young sheep), plus 20 suckler cows and their calves. Harry laboured in an unyielding landscape, with a fickle but generally cool climate. "Grass doesn't start to grow in a hurry up here!" he told me. Consequently, tupping time was delayed so that lambs were being born from about April 22.

I met Tommy Teasdale in the same area. He was born in Patterdale and his first job was as a shepherd in Hartsop, for which he was paid £18 for the half year, his meat (food) and lodging being provided by his employer. Tommy had in due course become a farmer and, like most Lakeland hill farmers, he had a ready wit. I heard that longevity must have something to do with the mountain air. He had a 33-year-old horse, a Dales cob bought as a three year-old at Penrith. "Some visitors asked me: 'How old's your horse?' And I told 'em: 'Hoss an' me's a hundred".

The least known dales must be those in Lakeland's Empty Quarter, southwards from Haweswater. A vast tract of fell and dale is in good hands, having become the largest Royal Society for the Protection of Birds reserve in England. Centred on Haweswater, it extends over 27,000 acres – which is some 5% of the National Park. The RSPB has entered into a wardening

FELL-GOING SHEEP BROUGHT DOWN TO WATENDLATH.

agreement with the Water Authority, who own the land. Conservation of bird life, including the celebrated nesting pair of golden eagles, will extend over an area bounded by High Street and Harter Fell, taking in Wet Sleddale, Swindale and the moors near Shap. The RSPB will manage the Naddle Low Woods, breeding place of pied flycatcher, redstart, great spotted and green woodpeckers.

Swindale ends with a wall of rock. Wet Sleddale merges into the moor but crags provide ravens with a choice of nesting sites and red deer join sheep at the grazings. Wet Sleddale is entered a little to the south of Shap. Manchester Corporation poured 125,200 cubic yards of concrete into the mouth of the valley and created a dam, the water from which flows through a tunnel to join Haweswater. The old Dales families were dispersed. The main beck rises on the lonely acres of Brown How, about 1,866 ft above sea level. After flowing northwards for a while, the beck makes a sudden turn and plunges down a staircase of black rock in the shadow of scars around which the ravens bark. For a few hundred yards, the beck swirls and tumbles in a deep gorge whose banks are lined by rowans.

It is hard now to recreate the life of the dale, for much has crumbled away. A ruined building known as Dale Head, and dating back to 1703, is believed to have been a school. New Ing was constructed at about the same time. Here lived the Noble family, one of whom, Lancelot, was sent with a message to the vicarage. He later reported to his mother that "t'priest's wrang in his heed … He said, 'where have you got your cap?' An', mudder, it was on my heed aw t'time".

In Wet Sleddale is a substantial reminder of man's craving for fresh meat in the long winter and one way in which a wealthy local family could satisfy it – by driving the native deer into a trap consisting of enclosures with high walls and killing the animals as required. The walls are gapped but stretches are at what must have been the full height, some 12ft. The driven deer would encounter the wall, follow it round and enter the enclosed area through an ingenious baffle. A second enclosure could have been the killing area. Thus did the Lowthers and their friends ensure a supply of good fresh meat during the long winter when most people had to be content with salted meat or no meat at all.

Sheep were at the centre of the Lakeland economy. Years ago, the farmers would kill off many old wethers (castrated males) and the flesh was dried, just like the ham of a pig. In Little Langdale, "we used to think that a three year old gelt ewe was the best mutton there was. When I was at home, in the bad years (1930s), I used to go round getting orders for wethers. We didn't bother to take 'em to Broughton mart or Ambleside fair, because it wasn't worth it. When the orders were in, fadder and me would set on and maybe kill two or three sheep in a week. He would stick 'em and I would skin 'em. We cured the legs. It would be getting on for a fortnight before the meat was ready. We hung the meat up in the 'beef baulk' (a special loft) above the fire. Cured mutton had a flavour of its own".

The stories of ordinary people interested me most. Life was generally hard. Girls fresh from school strove long and hard to keep up with an exacting domestic routine when hired for work at the farms. A Borrowdale man recalls: "My mother said that when she was a servant girl at High Lodore, she had to get up early in a morning and go out and wash in the trough. As mother was rushing about upstairs, having just got out of bed, Jane Wilson would shout: 'What's ta dewin', Laura?' 'Oh – I'se fastening me brat (apron)'. 'Nay', said Jane, 'fasten it when thou's coming downstairs – and lowse it when thou's going to bed'".

Herbert Grisedale, who was living at Elterwater when I first met him, recalled his young days in Great Langdale with zest and coherence. Herbert trudged from Middle Fell farmhouse to

Above – *The raven, sacred bird of the Norse folk, is thriving in the Lake District. It was the favourite species of Lakeland ornithologist Ernest Bleazard* (right). *He presided over the natural history collection at Tullie House, Carlisle.* Below – *A buzzard nest in a Lakeland oakwood.*

HIGH HAY BRIDGE, in the Rusland Valley, was the home in his later years of Herbert Fooks, one-time game warden for the Forestry Commission, and an authority on wild deer. He is seen here holding the "head" of a 30-stone Lakeland red deer. His widow developed the area into a nature reserve in his memory. Special protection is afforded the Furness red deer which, being woodlanders, and having good feed throughout the year, are the most impressive of the types of red deer to be found in Lakeland.

It was never intended to have deer in enclosures, but inevitably people brought in new-born deer they had found, and which they considered to have been deserted. This would not always have been the case. A roe kid recovered from the Windermere road was taken to Mrs. Fooks so that she might demonstrate her extraordinary skills at rearing young stock. A red deer calf collected by a family during a holiday in Scotland quickly matured and became a potential danger about the house. This stag became part of the Hay Bridge family.

Hay Bridge has for long had an educational role. Many people come to an understanding of country ways through visits to this quiet area of southern Lakeland.

school at Chapel Stile, a distance of three miles, though he missed school a good deal in the winter, when "'auld road used to flood". Thomas Fisher, the headmaster, was a man "good with a stick" who would deliver half a dozen strokes at a session. Herbert's schooldays ended when he was 14 years old. For the first summer, he worked at home. Then Anthony Chapman said he would like Herbert to help out at the *Old Dungeon Ghyll* during the winter. He received £6 and his food for six months hard labour on 56 acres, where 18 cattle and 10 sheep were kept. Mr. Chapman, then 90 years old, could still infuse life into local gatherings. Patrons who drank in the kitchen of an evening heard the old chap sing like a nightingale. "He had a beautiful voice", said Herbert.

Those were the days of really hard drinking. In extreme cases, a man would "go on the spree" and drink until he was senseless or had run out of money. A local man who liked to pour beer over his breakfast porridge told young Herbert: "Do that every day, and you'll grow up to be a man!" Another, who regularly visited Ambleside by horse-drawn trap, had so much to drink he returned home kneeling in the trap, from which he had to be assisted. The police presence was not very strong. "We had an old policeman; he must have been about 60 years old when I knew him". A "regular" at the *Old Dungeon Ghyll* who said he intended to walk over to Borrowdale for the week-end had too much too drink. He reached the top of Stake Pass, put his hand on a large stone and walked round and round that stone all night. Next morning, he returned to Langdale and resumed his drinking.

Jack Bland, who came to live in Kentmere in 1903, remembered the great days of Staveley sheep fair, held on October 7. The fair died out just before the 1914-18 war; it suffered competition from the auction marts. When Jack started work at Low Longmire Farm, Applethwaite, about 1890, he received £2 for the half year. "By gum, they'd screw their noses up if they got that for a week now. Aye, they'd want it for t'day – and then they wouldn't be satisfied, some on 'em!" (Like most other homes in Kentmere, Jack's place was built into the side of the hill and would not look out of place on a picture postcard with its white walls contrasting strongly with the raw, unadorned stone of the outbuildings. I saw a mass of honeysuckle spreading along the top of the garden wall. A sandy-coloured cat sat prim and composed at the gate).

In the mid-1950s, electricity reached as far up Kentmere as the diatomite works. The Haytons of Brow Top had installed a petrol engine to provide electrical power for their farm – a general farm which "incorporates everything but money". Already sheep farmers had turned from Herdwicks to Swaledales in the interest of greater profitability. The farmer and his son had worked hard to improve the outbuildings and "everything is now fully attested".

Water from a well was pumped into a cylinder at the top of the house and passed through the milk-coolers before returning to the well. The household supply of water came from another well, further up the hillside. A syphon lifted the water 20 feet to a piece of flat land before it ran down to the house. Joseph Hayton did the work in 1929. He told me that the upper spring had been located by a water-diviner.

I found pleasure in exploring the softer dales of the south. Rusland Valley, which opens its mouth to the mild breezes from Morecambe Bay, became for many years a place where I could savour the old-style Lakeland and its bountiful wildlife. It was at High Hay Bridge, near Booth, in 1971, that "Tissie" Fooks established a 220-acre nature reserve in memory of her late husband, Herbert, and to provide a sanctuary for the descendants of the Furness stock of red deer. For seven years I served on the Committee and joyfully attended meetings. Once, my attention strayed from the business in hand as I watched the gavortings of a red squirrel on a

Above – *A group photographed at Troutbeck School. One of the sad aspects of modern life is the decline in the number of rural schools, which were once a means of sustaining the rural community spirit.* Below – *Farmers attending Eskdale Show are wearing their "best setting off" clothes.*

shrub just outside the window of the building in which we were meeting. Badgers lumbered along their old tracks in the gloaming and once an otter's seal was found beside Rusland Pool.

The story of the Hay Bridge enterprise really began in Calcutta. It was here that Herbert Fooks grew up to an awareness of India's rich fauna. He became a dedicated and skilled naturalist. Always restless and never one for regular office hours, he returned to England, became a farmer, then keeper of the Royal waterfowl in St. James's Park and, in the early 1950s, a game warden for the Forestry Commission, based on Grizedale Forest in Lakeland. Herbert was responsible for training foresters in the scientific control of deer. These men took their new skills into all parts of Britain.

His widow vividly recalls the journey from London to Grizedale. It was a sudden move. The new accommodation was accepted without being seen. All their livestock was stacked in a caravan they towed north, and also in the caravan were their pets – ducks, bantams, canaries, exotic Indian birds, pigeons, dogs – all on free range! Hay Bridge was bought in December, 1957. At that time, High Hay Bridge was then just a shell. The farmhouse had burnt down last century, the barn was floorless, windowless and doorless. The new owners restored the barn, fitting plate glass where the doors had been so that the outward appearance of a barn was preserved. They put a wooden balcony overlooking a new pond for wildfowl. One mallard duck nested under a bench on the balcony for eight years; next year it decided to nest on a nearby wall.

This new house is set in a wild part of Lakeland. The horizon is crowned by a panorama of fells, including Coniston Old Man and Helvellyn. From the living room window, Tissie once observed eight wild roe at one time. She also saw 11 red deer on a bracken-covered knoll. When Herbert was alive, they witnessed from the same vantage point a red deer's spirited defence of her offspring, threatened by a fox. I recall staying overnight, and rising at dawn to wander down the woodland tracks to a high seat overlooking some of the 400 acres of the Rusland mosses, where roe deer were moving.

The Lyth Valley, drained by the Gilpin, has the soft beauty of flat fields and mosses. Large tracts of the valley used to spend so much time under water that a village was known as Brigsteer-by-the-Sea. Buttressing scars of white limestone – Whitbarrow, Scout Scar and Helsington Barrows – set off the valley. Outcropping limestone is excellent for stone fruit. If the Lyth Valley has any distinctive claim to fame among the dales of the North West, it is for its damsons. A myriad damson trees stand in massed ranks or spread themselves along the hedges. When they come into blossom, it is as though the area has been newly-dusted with snow. Twenty years ago, at Draw Well, one of 22 local farms where damsons were grown as a business venture, I heard about this delectable fruit from James Edward Inman, who then was 75 years old. He had planted most of the trees that stood in massed ranks round about the farm buildings. Each time I called I was impressed by the brightness of the farmhouse, under its thickening coat of whitewash. Edward Inman and I usually chatted in a stone-flagged room under an open timber ceiling, warmed by an aromatic wood fire.

As with other kinds of fruit, there are good years and poor years for damsons. Mr. Inman remembered a season when he and his brother searched hard and long, finding just enough damsons for a single pie. He had 700 fruit-bearing trees, the majority standing on a plot of ground handy to the house. He had known damson blossom to be as early as March 25 (this happened in 1922) and as late as May 12. Visitors used to flock to the Lyth Valley on Damson Sunday, when it was assessed that the blossom would be at its peak, making everything else look drab in comparison. The first damsons are harvested in early September. In good years, local

A LAKELAND SQUIRE   MAJOR HASELL, OF DALEMAIN, LOOKS AT THE OLDEST PART OF HIS HISTORIC HOME.

people sample their first fresh damson pies in late August. Having damson-loving friends in that district, I usually contrived to visit them at the beginning of September to taste one of their delicious damson pies. The farmers hired "pluckers" to help with the harvest. Up to the 1914-18 war, the rate for plucking was 3d for every 20lb gathered. "I've sold damsons in Kendal market at 6d a score pounds, after paying 3d to the plucker".

On some of my Lakeland trips I would meet Joseph Hardman, photographer, who lived at Kendal. Behind this bald statement is the fascinating story of a man from industrialised Lancashire, who began work as a "half-timer" at a factory producing shuttles for the cotton mill and who, in 1911, joyfully escaped to Kendal, where he found a menial job. Joseph became a member of the Kendal Photographic Society and, with a plate camera, took the first of many pictures of Lakeland life, his subjects included a farm man strewing grain in a Langdale field and a latter-day Viking attending to his Herdwick flock.

Joseph Hardman invariably appeared in the Lyth Valley at blossom time. He was to be seen at all the annual events in the shadow of the fells, and photographed the Shepherds' Meets at Mardale when they were held at the old *Dun Bull,* before Haweswater became a reservoir. Some of his best character studies were of Isaac Cookson, of Helton, who had attended Mardale meets for 61 years. An event of lesser importance than the great sporting events and farmers' gatherings, but one which had a strong appeal to Joseph, occurred in April when a large flock of sheep that had wintered on the Cartmel Fells was driven home to Hawes, in Wensleydale, over 40 miles away. The journey took two days. "Those sheep are kept to a strict timetable", he told me. "They pass Kendal Town Hall at twelve noon on the appointed day".

He and his wife once fled from the presence of a lively bull; they managed to clamber over a wall with seconds to spare – and had to wait for the bull to wander off before they could collect the contents of Mrs. Hardman's handbag, which she had dropped in their headlong flight. Joseph's greatest loss was a valuable camera, which fell into the tailwater of Skelwith Falls. He used plate cameras and often exposed five dozen plates in a day. A large number were topical and had to be posted off without delay. He never had a car, using a taxi or the car of a friend. "I think I can do better when I'm in the back of the car", he once told me. "I don't miss much then". His wife was his devoted assistant; he sometimes took along nurses from the Kendal hospital to add some glamour to his pictures.

The Lakeland dales claimed him for almost all the year, but he did like to spend a day or two at Berner's Close, Grange-over-Sands, and he usually had a week's holiday – at Blackpool! Much of his work is preserved in the archives of Abbot Hall at Kendal.

A COMMON EVENT OF THE LAKELAND SPRING.

THE FIRST FEW MINUTES IN THE LIFE OF A HERDWICK LAMB.

MY KNOWLEDGE of North Country ponies came from two Lakeland authorities. They were Miss Peggy Crosland, seen on the photograph, leading a pony near her home at Packway, near Windermere, and Jonty Wilson, the blacksmith of Kirkby Lonsdale. Miss Crosland's special joy was in keeping the Fell pony. Jonty enjoyed talking about the packhorse days, his grandfather having had a string of animals, mainly the type now known as the Dales pony, which is slightly bigger than the Fell. Grandfather's team of ponies moved goods for one of the contractors building the Settle-Carlisle railway.

Jonty was fond of talking about the Galloway Gate, an early version of the M6, the Gate extending for some 130 miles from lowland Lancashire through eastern Lakeland into south-west Scotland. "Galloway" was the name given to a cob seen commonly on the farms, where it was the "maid of all work". A farmer would say to his son, when some hard work had to be done: "Git in t'auld Gallowa'."

Kendal was an important terminus for packhorses. It has been estimated that over 300 animals left the town each working day. Some journeyed into Yorkshire. Others were directed as far off as London. Packhorse trains reached Kendal from as far as Wigan and Whitehaven, Barnard Castle and Cockermouth. Two groups arrived from Penrith twice a week and there was a similar service from Hawkshead.

Horses and ponies served man from early times until the transport revolution. Within living memory, ponies and cobs were being reared for local use or to be sold to tradesmen in the towns. A writer about Grasmere in 1875 met a man whose grandmother remembered the arrival of new bells for the church; they were transported over White Moss, borne on sleds drawn by ponies. It is said that the lead needed for roofing work at Windermere church was moved from Whitehaven on ponyback.

RURAL OCCUPATIONS

AT "PACKWAY", the home of Miss Peggy Crosland, near Windermere, I met Rufus, a fell pony born and bred on the fells beyond Heltondale. Rufus was untouched by human hands for the first three years of his life. He was then captured and broken in. At the time I met the black pony, he was 14 years of age. In his varied working life, he had carried a shepherd and been used at the Calgarth trekking centre. For some years he had been owned and well-cared-for by the Crosslands. Peggy was for many years secretary of the Fell Pony Society.

One wintry day, at "Packway", I took part in the regular journey over Packway Lot to an isolated building from which hay is distributed to the brood mares and corn to a flock of assorted hens. To Rufus, the sure-footed 13.3 h.h. pony, a load of hay and some hen food was as nothing. I asked Peggy how much weight Rufus could take and she said, smilingly, that the main problem was how much she could manage to lift on to his back!

The Crosslands once had their own meadow lower down the hill and, making hay by hand methods, they laboriously transported it up to "Packway" on the backs of their fell ponies. The house lies beside an old packhorse track leading from the Ferry below Bowness to Kendal, roughly parallel but to the west of the Crook-Kendal road. Peggy told me about Kendal's former importance as a terminus for packhorses. It has been estimated that over 300 animals left the town each working day, some journeying into Yorkshire and others as far as London. There would be about 20 ponies in a team. Packhorse traffic between the lake and Kendal declined in the closing years of the 18th century. A turnpike road was constructed, making wheeled traffic possible.

Peggy told the story of an old man who operated a train of pack animals on a route that took in the high passes of Wrynose ("pass of the stallion") and Hardknott to Ravenglass. The team was led by a black stallion which knew the way. The man rode on horseback but if the wayside halt was an inn he let the stallion lead off the other animals and settled down to more drinking. Mounting his horse, he would then overtake the packhorses before they reached the next inn, where the process was repeated.

The fell pony was the "fell galloway" of the hill farmer. In fact, the Galloway breed (once kept on each side of the Solway) is extinct, said Peggy. "People got to calling any small horse a galloway". Ponies still live in a semi-wild state along the East Fellside of the northern Pennines and groups are spread about the hills between Pooley Bridge and the head of Kentmere. Ponies cross High Street and High Raise, where they are as much at home as the sheep. Some fell ponies have spent 18, even 20 years, without a halter. Black, brown and bay are the principal shades. Dark-coloured ponies are easier to see than light stock. In winter, fell ponies may condescend to champ some hay. I watched a group near Helton in March; they had wisely descended from the high fells as the "snow dogs" began to howl.

Many ponies were once to be seen in Lakeland. A farmer on the eastern fells would keep two or three mares and breed from them. Ponies were put between shafts. Colts were bought by

The Fell Pony in Lakeland. Above – At Hilton, on the East Fellside near Appleby. Below – At "Packway", near Windermere, where the animal was being foddered by Miss Peggy Crosland. Such ponies run in a semi-wild state on the fells above Haweswater and also on the Northern Pennines.

colliery owners and went down the pits. The demand fell away, until – about 1924 – one Lakeland breeder was selling an animal that had been broken in to drive for as little as £44. The trade picked up in the early 1950s with the increasing popularity of pony trekking. Farmers who specialise in breeding ponies are naturally proud of their stock but I was not expecting the reply I received when I asked one breeder how long his family had kept ponies. He said: "Grandfather used to have them". There was a pause, and he added: "... and maybe his grandfather!"

At Bousfield, near Orton, in the 1950s, I met William Hully who – I was assured – knew a lot about horses; he had attended Brough Hill horse fair for over 70 years. He described his home as being "just on the division between Clydesdales and Shires". William was 88 years old when we conversed. He started riding horses as a lad. When he was 21 years old he "found" *Comet*, the 11 cwt stallion that decided his career. That stallion became an entire (an uncastrated animal used for breeding). "I led him for 20 years on the same piece of ground, and he was serving over 160 mares a season". The famous animal could trot a mile in three minutes. "You know, I never had a pony that could gallop as fast as old *Comet* could trot!"

William Hully remarked: "I started wi' nowt, an' no-one left me owt". He "nobbut went to Orton School, and they say I'm one o' t'best writers – an' no glasses either!" During the 1914-18 war he bought horses for the Army. He was in his "second hundred" when the Armistice came. William was never one to "throw brass about". When John Lloyd, a local dealer, advised him to "buy the best" he had replied: "Aye, I would, but my pocket troubles me!"

Before the 1914-18 war, a good horse could be bought from between £40 and £50. The war pushed up the price to over £100. In Lakeland, Clydesdales were always popular. They did not have as much hair on their legs and did not collect the dirt as much as a Shire horse. It took two or three months to break in a horse for farm work. The horse had to become accustomed to having a bit in its mouth. It was then introduced to the saddle and to tracings for work with implements. Sometimes an old pair of trousers, filled with straw, was strapped to a horse's back, to simulate a rider, and for tracings to be effective an animal was yoked to a log to see if it could pull. Farm servants had to fodder the horses at the start of a new day; they must also feed and groom the working horses at the end of the day. Now, as a retired farmer told me, "a man just gets off a tractor and he's finished".

Many farmhouses stand in grand isolation, surrounded by the best of Lakeland scenery. Hartsop Hall, near Brotherswater, has long been the home of the Allen family, latterly as tenants of The National Trust. The white-washed farmhouse looks tiny when set against the majesty of the crags and wooded fells but at close range the buildings are seen to be substantial. J.W. Allen told me that the oldest part dates from the 16th century. "The place was originally built as a stopping-off place for the monks travelling from Furness Abbey to Lanercost Priory". The National Trust's ownership of about 80 dalehead farms ensures there will be no unsightly developments, nor a departure from traditional forms of farming. Yew Tree Farm, beside the road from Coniston to Skelwith Bridge, is one of Lakeland's many characterful 17th century structures. It also remains a workaday farm, dedicated to the raising of "suckler" cattle and hill sheep. Both Herdwick and Swaledale breeds are represented here. I have had many a "crack" with the tenants, Jean and Daniel Birkett. Yew Tree Farm comes under the gaze of Wetherlam, which a 19th century writer described as "the Old Man's stupendous brother", but the Yew Tree sheep run on Holme Fell, grazing among the rocks and bracken patches.

Yew Tree Farm has a huge barn with a so-called spinning gallery. Was this once-common Lakeland feature really used for spinning, despite the popular notion of spinsters sitting here to process wool? Others claim this gallery was just a convenient means of access to a higher level. Under the barn's capacious roof is stacked the winter fodder for the stock.

When I first met the Richardsons of Gatesgarth (Buttermere) in 1967, they had four stocks of Herdwicks, totalling 2,500 sheep. Eight dogs helped with the gathering but only three men were available to do the sheep-clipping and attendant jobs – re-marking the animals and dipping them against the summer fly pests. This month-long job began in June, the men working in the old salving house, in which, each autumn, many years before the flockmaster and his men had patiently and methodically parted a sheep's wool and applied a mixture of tar and grease to the skin.

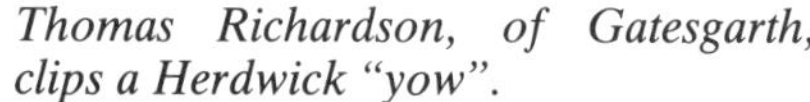

Thomas Richardson, of Gatesgarth, clips a Herdwick "yow".

HERDWICK RAMS AT KESWICK SHOW.

Now the building contained a large pen of sheep fresh from the fells. A dry day had been chosen, for damp wool becomes foisty and begins to smell. Thomas Richardson clipped off the fleece in time-honoured fashion, putting a sheep on its back so that he might start shearing at a foreleg ("some people begin with t'neck"). The shears were set to work down the side of the animal towards a hind leg and tail. The wool was then clipped from the area of the stomach and Thomas repeated the process on the other side, by which time the sheep was half sitting, staring about with large bright eyes but, in the hands of a master shearer, remaining calm. A tup, which is usually clipped first, and yields 10lb of wool against the 3lb or 3½lb of the ewe, is treated with special respect. "A tup can get its horns in about your ribs". A fleece was smoothed, rolled, wrapped using a twisted piece of the wool and put to one side to be stored against the time it was collected by the lorry from the merchant.

With the fleece went the sheep marks, which distinguished Mr. Richardson's Gatesgarth sheep from others, so the animal must be re-marked, for the Richardson sheep edged up to flocks from Wasdale, Ennerdale, Borrowdale, Newlands and Loweswater. Tar was once used for marking, but this would not easily scour out at the mills. It was interesting to see the special Gatesgarth mark – a red "pop". A Scale Force sheep was given a stroke of red down the far side and a "pop" on the near side, while Burtness stock sported a "stroke" down the far ribs.

Sheep suffered from ailments with quaint names – blackleg, braxey, pulpy kidney, liver fluke. Such diseases were brought under control by veterinary science in a matter of 30 years. Sidney Cole said that in the 1920s the only cure for fluke on damp pastures was to keep ducks, which ate up the snails that were part of the fluke's life cycle. "It helped a bit – but it was nothing out of the ordinary to lose 20 per cent of the flock from liver fluke".

Another dreaded infection, especially in a humid summer, was "the fly" or an infestation by the maggots of the green bottle fly. While this was a great trouble and cause of loss to all sheep farmers, it was especially so on the fells. Many "heafs" were six and seven miles from the farm and it was possible to see the sheep only once a week. "In thundery weather, it was nothing unusual to find half a dozen dead and 20 or 30 'struck' out of 200. The time taken to dress the affected sheep wounds was a serious matter coming, as it nearly always did, in the middle of haytime". Remedial measures were found. "The fly" was mastered by DDT dips, which in course of time were shown to have injurious effects on other creatures. The once high Lakeland population of peregrine falcons was greatly depleted and when such dips were prohibited, the falcon recovered its former status.

Some Lakeland sheep used to carry bells around their necks; the clanking sound gave an alpine flavour to many a desolate stretch of countryside. Visit a fell farm up to the 1914-18 war, and you would find a flock of wethers (emasculated males) following the high ground; they would be wintered in low country, for a few shillings a head, and in spring be moved back to the farm to fatten up for the butcher, being sold about August. The leading wether wore the bell. With several groups of males in one district, the sound of each bell was distinctive, which helped the farmer at gathering time.

A highlight of any visit to Great Langdale was to have a "crack" with Joseph Gregg. He told me that the shepherd of 60 and more years ago received as little as £1, sometimes £1.5s a week and worked unnumbered hours in all weathers. Talk of money prompted Joseph to recall the inter-war Slump. In 1927, a ewe was bringing £2, but four years later he was not able to sell his ewes for 10s each. "There were no subsidies then". The price of sheep did not pick up until the next war, and when grading of stock began at the marts only 1s.2d a lb was being allowed.

A TOP QUALITY Herdwick ram is pictured here. It was photographed at a farm near Thirlmere. The slatted floor of a building constructed mainly for the wintering of sheep allows sheep droppings to get clear. Slatting on the walls allows air to circulate, while restricting the entry of rain and snow.

It was once customary to drive young sheep from the fell farms to low country for their first winter. So they avoided the rigours of snow and ice

in high places. The mossland along the sea-edge of Cumbria held a large number of wintering Lakeland sheep. Driving the stock to and from the wintering grounds on foot could be a prolonged task.

Herdwick rams, or "tips", as the men of western Lakeland call them, were hired not bought by a farmer. This happened in the autumn. The rams were returned to the owners on an appointed day in the spring.

Joseph said that sheep farming was at its best financially in 1955, since when it had "gone downwards".

Conversation soon turned to Herdwick sheep. He had attended Mardale Shepherds' Meet for a few years before the 1914-18 war. The Meet was intended for the return of any stray sheep. He had driven sheep from Kentmere to Mardale. "We did a fair bit of droving at one time. We helped one another. No one expected to be paid. I drove tups from Eskdale Show to Mardale and Longsleddale". Tups were hired, put to work on the ewes to ensure a "change of blood" and returned to the owner. Two famous events for hiring tups were Eskdale Show, held towards the end of September, and Keswick Back End Fair, in early October. The tups were returned to Eskdale and Keswick at special events in the following May. "You could get a good tup for £1, but now (1974) they ask you a fairish price. A tup with a good character will cost £5 for the season".

Joseph was keen to promote Herdwick wool for making cloth. "It has only one fault – it lasts too long", he told me. "One year I got 8lb of wool off a sheep and sent the wool to a firm in the north that specialises in making up suits. My suit was as good as a raincoat. I walked from Eskdale to catch the morning bus at Elterwater. I went on to Kendal, then returned to Elterwater. When I'd left the bus I'd to walk over Wrynose and Hardknott passes. It was raining all the time. At the end of the walk, I took off the Herdwick suit and just shook it. That suit was as dry as when I set off!"

Then it was back to sheep. "We don't want sheep in the Lake District if they have soft wool. And we don't want the wool too hard. A sheep should have a decent 'jacket' with a bit o' waistcoat in it to keep the storm out". A Herdwick would stand a fair amount of weather. "And so does a sheep farmer!" On March 27, 1919, Joseph was helping to put some gaps up (he had to carry stones a long way up the fell before he could start walling) and "we decided to have dinner. We sat down to have our packed meals. There wasn't a cloud in the sky. We couldn't have had a finer March day. Then the sheep started moving down the fellside. They were all bleating. It was a sign of a coming storm. By the time we had finishing dinner, it was snowing, out of a blue sky it seemed. Before we got home it had put down six or seven inches of snow and it was blowing it. We'd not been long at home when we had to turn out with a dog to pull sheep out of drifts".

John James Mitchell, of Stool End, Great Langdale, told me: "Our sheep are terribly cunning when there's a blizzard. They travel to the hill ends; they seem to know that the wind will blow the snow of these places. They never get into the hollows where snow will cover them up. A lot of 'em make straight for the farm ..." Harry Wilson, of Tarn Foot, near Loughrigg Tarn, recalled the 1947 blizzard when many sheep were lost and had to be sought in the

Three fine knitting sticks from the old Westmorland/Yorkshire border area.

GROOMING A HERDWICK SHEEP BEFORE IT ENTERS THE SHOW RING, ESKDALE.

THE HERDWICK: DISTINCTIVE SHEEP BREED OF LAKELAND.
This study of a Herdwick ram shows the "frosty" appearance of the face.

Above, left – *Young Herdwicks at Seath-waite, head of Borrowdale.* Right – *Clipping a sheep by hand.* Left – *Lambing time in Lortonvale. Many of the sheep terms used in Lakeland are Norse in origin.*

snowdrifts. Whin bushes (gorse) that had been overswept by snow became death traps. Sheep, breaking through the crust on the snow, were caught by the branches and were found "hanging like apples". The farmers and their dogs went out looking for sheep. "It was not a matter of how many we'd find alive – but how many had died". At lambing time, a farmer going his rounds with a companion on a cold, wet morning commented: "It's a real tickler". In such weather, it was vital for a lamb to take milk from the ewe as quickly as possible. If it had some difficulty, the ewe was turned and firmly held. The lamb was put into position to suck and was then tickled at the tail root, stimulating it to drink.

Herbert Grizedale worked at Middle Fell, Langdale, and shared the supervision of a flock of 1,200 Herdwicks which grazed the Pikes, High Whitestone and "on towards Thirlmere". Five or six times a year, the men went out to rescue sheep that had become cragfast. Herbert had taken "many a dozen" sheep out of Gimmer Crag, Harrison Stickle, Raven Crag and other rock faces. He told me that a team of three men undertook this sort of work. They needed a hempen "crag rope" about 60 feet long, and a finer "draw rope" with which to lasso the sheep when the man on the main rope was close to the animal.

The man on the rope – and that was usually Herbert – carried a pocket full of small stones. When he was dangling about eight feet above the sheep, he pitched stones on either side of the ledge. The sheep was thus reminded of the drop. Otherwise, becoming scared in the presence of people, it might have jumped off the ledge. A stick was a vital part of the equipment. A nail driven in near the end stopped the lighter "draw rope" from slipping off. The stick was used like a fishing rod and the noosed rope was dangled over the sheep and then slipped over its head. The rescuer fastened the animal's legs together and, clutching the struggling creature, was drawn up the crag face by his friends. "A lot of thought went into rescuing a cragfast sheep. Sometimes we'd disturb a fox and watch it scamper away ..."

Herbert recalled when a butcher paid about £1 for a 40lb wether sheep. He himself had slaughtered dozens of Herdwicks and hawked the mutton around Elterwater and Chapel Stile at 6d a lb. He once sold a dressed fowl to a woman for 2s. She exclaimed: "My, isn't it dear?" Some mutton was salted down for the winter. "Salted leg", dangling from the beams of a Lakeland farm kitchen, was once a familiar sight. "You put a little bit of saltpetre on the bone end, and salt on the flesh. We lived on 'hot pots' and 'tatie hashes' in those days!" Joseph Gregg's mother made a favourite dish with bits of fatty Herdwick mutton. It was called Sweet Pie. "We always had it at Christmas, and we didn't want much at a time. It's the best pie I've ever tasted. Mother used a big dish and she put a thin crust over the pie".

Fred Barker, of Patterdale, demonstrated how to make a shepherd's crook. When he carries a crook on to the fell, the Lakeland shepherd has the equivalent of three legs. The crook is deftly used to catch sheep or lambs. Fred gathered hazel from local woods at the "back-end" of the year. It was then that "t'saps out on 't". The wood was put in a cool but draughty place to season. A tup horn picked up on the fell became the crook itself. The supply was augmented by irregular horns that were proving troublesome to tups and had to be sawn off. Boiling the horn softened it sufficiently for it to be shaped into the traditional shape. In attaching the crook to its shaft, he drilled a hole five-eighths of an inch thick into the horn and inserted the wood. A ring of deer horn acted as a ferrule. Unnumbered winter hours were devoted to carving. Fred reckoned that a shepherd's crook should not be too ornate. The bone was burnt with a hot iron to get a brown colouring and with black enamel and white lacquer to make any carvings life-like. The carving itself was done merely with rasp and knife. If anything, modern crooks are too elaborate. Every hill farmer needed a dog. Joseph Relph, a trainer of outstanding sheepdogs

Above – *A pint at the "local"*. Right – *Line-up of horses from the Elterwater gunpowder works*. Below – *Folk-dancing, which was especially popular in the 1930s.*

who lived at Birkett Bank, Threlkeld, was mentioned with respect wherever sheepdog men gathered. He took his first dog to a trials field when he was in his early "twenties" and the joy of working dogs in competitive conditions remained with him to the end of his life. He had twice won the doubles championship at the English National. Joe remembered the names of his dogs in threes, and he told me of some of the early animals he owned – Tuss, Lady and Mack; Bright, Jack and Kip; Fleet, Jack and Kip.

At Bampton, near Shap, I watched John Bowman and his son, also named John, building a stone wall in which there was not a dab of mortar. I saw them manoeuvre an immense limestone "through" into place. A Lakeland drystone wall is really two walls in one, side by side, the whole tapering slightly, and it is bound together by the "throughs" that extend from one side of the wall to the other. The wall on which the Bowmans were working would be five feet high, plus another seven inches or so for the topstones, known as "cams". When topstones lie side by side, obliquely, a wall is said to have a "cammed top". If alternating tall and short stones are used, it has a "rough top". In some parts of Lakeland this style is known as "cock and hen". Joseph Harrison, of Brotherilkeld, Eskdale, had 15 miles of drystone walls on his farm and devoted at least three weeks out of every year to their maintenance. Most of the gaps appear in walls when there is a thaw after frosty weather. He said: "When you see a wall shutter in a hard spell, you know it is going to thaw!" At Yew Tree Farm, north of Coniston, Daniel Birkett told me that the local stone may literally go rotten, shattered by extremes of temperature, by wind and rain. The now useless stone is replaced with quarry stone. Elsewhere, Daniel Birkett replaces old stone field drains that have become worn with modern tile drains. A farm which looks ageless, keeps its good looks and neat apperance through the farmer's hard work and the attention given to the fabric of the buildings by the landlord, in this case The National Trust.

Material for the Lakeland walls were usually freestone (secured at small handy quarries) and slate (which is slow and tedious to use). Stone for the walls running to the fell-tops, enclosing the "intakes", would have to be sledded, the sleds drawn by Galloways (sure-footed ponies). A good waller, who could built seven yards a day, was said never to pick up a particular stone more than once. Sidney Cole, of Caldbeck, believed that the last Lakeland fell to be enclosed with walls was Binsey, near Ruthwaite. Towards the end of last century, father and three sons built a three-mile long wall. A local farmer remarked, as they began, that they would never meet again in this world because two built one way and two the other way round the fell. One of the wallers died during the five years it took to complete the work.

Right – *Whitewashing the wall of a Lakeland farm. By using whitewash rather than paint, the walls are permitted to "breathe". Below – Preparing to repair a lakeside wall on the east side of Coniston Water.*

THE HEAD of Glenridding valley, in the Ullswater area, was scarred and battered by almost 200 years of intensive mining. Our photograph shows the mine buildings as they were towards the end of the mining period.

The commercial exploitation of lead near Ullswater dated mainly from the latter part of the 18th century. By 1959, the labour force was down to 50, which was a quarter of the wartime total. The limited amount of ore that remained was of low grade and could not be economically worked. Almost 40 years ago there was a world-wide recession in lead-mining. The Mine closed in 1961. Use was found for some of the buildings. What was a hostel for miners became one of the Lakeland group of Youth Hostels.

DANGER: MEN AT WORK

IN A SMALL cottage on a hill above Coniston Water, I watched two brass candlesticks blink in the strong sunlight that slanted across the mantelpiece. On the fire below, a kettle was singing quietly to itself, held in place by a hook which hung down from a well-polished "reckon". The old lady who had been sitting on the left of the fireplace walked over to the sideboard and brought a thin strip of metal for my inspection. It was only a common metal, of no great value, but the smile on her face and the tone of her voice suggested that she treasured it greatly. It was a piece of copper – mined at Coniston.

It is well-known that up to the 1914-18 war, copper was mined in the fells above Coniston. In 1952, there were still many people with exciting tales of an industry that gave the village more than local fame. George Stephens, then 82 years old, recalled when an experienced worker received about a guinea a week. When he started at the mines, he was aged 11 and received 4s a week. At its peak, a little over a century ago, Lakeland mining employed about 1,000 men. A miner in this area had a chancy occupation, being at the whims of the market. As the price of minerals fell, mines were closed and the worker prepared to move elsewhere. This mobility of labour led some people to take jobs abroad. Thomas Shaw, whose first jobs were at Coniston, twice went to the American Rockies. "A lot of men went from Coniston to America", his son, W.T. (Bill) Shaw told me. "Some men came back. Others stayed in the New World".

The Lakeland world of Bill Shaw, was that of the mine – deep, dark, dank but as exciting as Aladdin's Cave to those who dedicated themselves to locating and extracting of minerals. Bill was born at Coniston in 1909, when the village was about half its present size. It was a workaday village. Men had their sleeves rolled up and their faces were dusty from working at the slate quarries. The largest quarry, on the face of Coniston Old Man, was owned by the Mandale brothers, who employed about 100 men and boys. "Because they were able to get a decent-sized slate, there was a good market, particularly in the towns lower down Lancashire". A complex of quarries could be found at Tilberthwaite.

Coniston was best known for its ancient copper mines. Bill Shaw could recall when a French company operated there. "They came before the 1914-18 war, intent on opening the mines in a big way. First, they were to work through the old mine dumps and the plant was said to have cost them £30,000. My father came back into the district to help with the work. The venture never came to anything. The last underground mining was in 1908". This effort by the French ended with the outbreak of war. "We in Coniston were familiar with the sight of Count Henri de Varnie, the engineer. He was a rare person in those days – a man who could fly an aircraft. When war started, he was called up into the French Air Force. He was shot down and died. Count Henri used to stay at the *Waterhead Hotel* in Coniston. It was then the main hotel. When I was about five years old, my family was living across the lake from Coniston, but I remember being taken to the mines – and seeing this romantic French count".

Above – *Bill Shaw, latterly of Chestnut Hill, Keswick, an authority on the Lakeland mining industry. Below – A "river" of Lakeland slate, pictured in a shed at Spout Crag.*

The last attempt to open up the copper mines came in the mid-1950s, when the price of copper was good. Before anything could be developed, that price had tumbled again, this time to below £300 a ton. Bill Shaw believed there was a good deal of copper left. "I have never seen it, but the old people told me this was so. Members of my own family supported this view". By the late 1920s, a new slate quarry had been opened at Broughton Moor, near Coniston. It was to become the major employer of labour. In the inter-war years, the slate quarryman made a reasonable wage. He worked on contract and received about £2, according to the quantity of slate produced. Small gangs – each of four men – reached mutually satisfying arrangements with the agent.

Bill Shaw was an entertaining companion, either at his home in Chestnut Hill, Keswick, or "in the field", where he could be relied upon to find traces of t'Owd Man, as past generations of miners were collectively known. At least five generations of the Shaw family worked in the Lakeland mines. Bill Shaw was born at Coniston, worked in the local mines and then had a good deal of experience in those of Patterdale. I persuaded Bill to enlarge some research he had done into the mines of the Coniston area, and this was published as *Mining in the Lake Counties*. Another time, he took me to Brandlehow, on the western side of Derwentwater, and told me about a mine which is thought to have been started in the days of the first Elizabeth and closed when the price of lead slumped about 1890.

A 500 ft deep shaft had been excavated close to the lake and during the heyday of the mine between 70 and 80 men were employed. According to Postlethwaite, the annual production was 300 tons of dressed lead ore a year, and this tallied with what Bill Shaw had discovered from old documents. I heard that an overshot waterwheel, 30 feet in diameter, propelled machinery that crushed and dressed the ore. A steam engine installed in 1888 was of 350 h.p. and could be operated at a depth of 200 fathoms. Brandlehow was a fairly wet mine by Lakeland standards, and this was not just connected with its proximity to the lake. "A spring followed them down all the way. The old miners had a lot of water from the top to the bottom. The deep-seated water was saline". We rummaged among small spoil heaps, collecting some fragments of galena and zinc. "Odd specimens of fluorspar have been found", said Bill, "and that's a fairly rare mineral in the Lake District proper".

In distant times, when Lakeland was wracked by volcanoes, a great fissure opened on the eastern side of what was to become Helvellyn. Into the fissure poured mineral solutions from the depths of the earth, and galena was predominant. Galena is a lead sulphite containing 70 to 80 per cent of pig lead metal, six ounces of silver per ton of galena and the rest mostly sulphur. It was, in fact, a lead vein, dipping about 70 degrees to the east in a NNE direction. For some years after I began to edit *Cumbria* magazine, I could chat with men who were working the vein some 3,000 feet below ground. Greenside Mine, Glenridding, has long since been closed and the area was landscaped to remove the worst eyesores.

From the first feeble scratchings on the ground, miners blasted and shovelled their way around and along the mineral vein and raised slagheaps like minor pyramids, testifying to their energy. The men changed the courses (and colour) of the local streams; they built rows of cottages at Glenridding. The mine itself remained decently out of sight of the main road near Ullswater. Matterdale farmers in a small way worked at the Greenside lead mines. Joseph Bell told me: "They'd perhaps go to Greenside on a Sunday night, taking with them plenty of food, and return home on Friday. Their families managed their little farms in their absence. If a man had a good week at the mines, he'd return home with 18s or £1 in his pocket". Some of the old-time miners walked 34 miles from Alston to their work at Greenside; they had four or five days'

GREENSIDE MINING COMPANY brought habitations to the lonely Glenridding valley. An acute milk shortage was experienced in the area, and so the company added farming to its activities. Miners might be called away from their jobs to help with the harvest. In 1864, Gillside Farm was taken over, with its flock of 260 Herdwick sheep, at a yearly rental of £120.

Plans were made to convert Gillside into a milk farm and it was still in the company's hands in 1931. A haymaking account showed that in 1882 John Norman put in two day's haymaking, a total of 34½ hours, and was paid £1.5.3d.

A full-time shepherd, Thomas Salkeld, was appointed in 1884. He tramped the fells with his dog and was given the princely sum of £1 a week. Isaac Blamire attended to the horses at the mine. Every summer he would lead two of the most powerful animals down the rutted road to Gillside and harness them to the mowing machine.

supply of food in sacks on their backs. The bothy in which they were accommodated became the mine office. A hostel built in 1937 and containing 20 bedrooms is now well used as a YHA hostel.

During the 1914-18 war, workers were brought in from Penrith and Threlkeld. Italian prisoners, straight from the deserts of North Africa, worked in the mine and were quartered in a special camp. In 15 years, the underground labour force had shrunk from 200 to 40. The remaining miners travelled to work along the Lucy Level, which was about seven feet high and six feet wide. They had at least a mile to travel to their work. During the 1939-45 war, the Greenside men, working round the clock, provided Britain with five-sevenths of all the lead mined in the country.

Once the Greenside miners used candles for illumination. They worked patiently, each job being protracted. Hammer and steel bar were used to drill a hole 12 to 18 inches long to hold a charge of black powder. Modern workers were slicing through five to six feet of material in a shift and employing gelatine dynamite if even greater effort was desired. Initially, ore was transported on the backs of horses to the Keswick area to be smelted. Then the smelting and de-silvering processes were carried out on the site of the mine. In the 1950s, ore was being taken by road to Newcastle, about 95 miles away.

Cyril Connor, the manager of Greenside in 1957, told me the modern story of a mine which, some said, had first been worked by the Romans. Eighty per cent of the Glenridding male population was employed at the mine and 53 of the local houses belonged to the Company, which caused Glenridding to develop rapidly at a time when the old tourist centre was Patterdale. As I walked to Mr. Connor's house in a darkness broken only by a few public lights and the illumination cast from the windows of miners' homes – through curtains of floral pattern – I saw the lights of Greenside Mine shining at the head of the valley. Two shifts were organised. The work was continuous, from 8 a.m. until midnight. Rock was broken into fine fragments and then rolled down wooden chutes into steel wagons, which were hoisted up two shafts of a total height of 1,000 feet to the Lucy Level and the surface. Electric battery locomotives then took over the wagons for the last stretch of the journey, though until 12 years before, ponies had been used for this work. Power for the enterprise came from hydro electric power stations installed in 1928. One of the "reservoirs" was Red Tarn, in the shadow of mighty Helvellyn. The Top Dam lay at the side of Sticks Pass, 1,000 feet above the mine buildings.

As the manager spoke, I thought of the huge dumps of waste material. He said that 2,500 tons of lead ore a month was being drawn from Greenside Mine. Only 150 tons were lead concentrates. The remainder, classified as waste and known as "tailings", was dumped on the fellside. In the process of extracting 150 tons, seven tons of water were needed for every ton of ore.

The Greenside Mine closed at 3 p.m. on a Wednesday in late January, 1961. One of its last roles was research by the Atomic Energy Commission into the effects of underground explosions. At Greenside, these were modest affairs, aimed at dislodging a few tons of rock. An old friend, Mr. Oglethorpe, who began work at the lead mine when he was 16 years and rose from apprentice to chief engineer, had the sad task of locking up. "I delivered the keys of the office to the secretary, who was tidying up for the last time. He took the keys to a solicitor at Penrith – and that was that". After the closure, some mine houses changed hands at only £300. Huts erected to accommodate Italian prisoners of war became part of the youth hostel. With lead no longer being produced at Greenside, there followed one of the largest clean-up operations the Lake District has seen. The mining scars are being healed.

Slate quarrying, old and new. Left – *This man-made cavern at Elterwater testifies to the incredible energy of quarrymen who were seeking the best quality material. Quarrying was merged with mining as they went underground! Below – An impressive vehicle used for quarrying at Spout Crag, above Great Langdale.*

Quarrying for slate is one of Cumbria's oldest traditional occupations. Slate was used to roof a traditional farmstead and cottage. It provided material for walls, which in a large part explains why the old style of building so perfectly compliments the landscape. More recently, Lakeland slate has been used to clad some of the world's newest and most imposing buildings. An industry that was labour intensive is now run by a few men, using big machines. '

Elterwater quarry has some yawning holes leading into underground workings which are now disused. When I met the general manager, George Baines, in 1972, he told me that slagheaps had been considerably reduced in size, thousands of tons of rock having been carted out for road improvements on Dunmail Raise and between Staveley and Kendal. In the old days, little else but roofing slates were produced. From the Welsh quarries came slates of uniform size, but the products of a Westmorland quarry were individualistic, the slates being of random widths and many qualities.

Gunpowder, once produced at a small factory at Elterwater, was the preferred explosive, for it has a slower expansion rate than such an explosive as gelignite. Quarrying was all handwork, with the men using the laborious system of hand – docking blocks of slate into convenient sizes for splitting; they then dressed the pieces by hand. I mentioned the subterranean workings. George Baines told me that the office in which we chatted lay above an enormous man-made cavern which was serving the quarry well. "All our sludge from the machines comes through one outlet into the settling tanks. When the tanks are full of solids, a pump transfers the solids into the cavern. Surplus water is filtered by the ancient spoil heaps. The water is clean by the time it reaches the river". Green slate of fine quality was won in Kentmere, where at one time 40 quarrymen worked on the surface or underground. The fell has been honeycombed. When in 1955 I met Jack Williams, who with his brother William owned the quarries, only three quarrymen were being employed. The art of "riving" or splitting slate had not been mechanised. The best quality slates supplied from Kentmere were "four to the inch". Years ago, barracks large enough to accommodate 20 men were built at the quarries. Some of the men left the site once a month, for a "real old spree" at Staveley. The inn at Kentmere had been closed down by the law because of heavy drinking and immorality. Up to the beginning of this century, blue slate was quarried by opencast means on the fellside near Kentmere Hall. Lower down the valley, men once mined for lead.

I have never tired of watching a man splitting slate. The appeal lay in the skilful co-ordination of mind, eye and hand. John Taylor, who worked the green slate of Honister, picked up a piece of slate several inches thick, placed it on end and, from a sitting position, rested a chisel along the grain and then rapped the top of the chisel with a hammer. With a few deft strokes he would split the slate again and again – and again. His workplace was a roomy shed just off the Honister Pass. He devoted his working day to reducing over half a ton of large pieces of slate into the fine, smooth slates for which there was a considerable demand both in Britain and places overseas.

John had started work at the top quarries on Coniston Old Man, to which he and the many other workers walked daily. The finished material was brought down the hill by horse and cart, with a sled attached to the cart to act as a brake, affording a greater measure of control. About 100 men worked at that quarry, which went out of business largely as the result of a change of fashion. It turned out grey slate, hard and durable. Then more and more customers found green slate more attractive. John went to Broughton Moor quarry, thence (in 1949) to Honister. A piece of slate in his capable hands yielded roofing slates at the rate of four to just over the inch. The chisel used was made to a width equivalent to the thickness of eight slates. John did not need to check measurements. He worked "by t'rack o' t'eye" but with great precision.

A visitor to Honister marvels at the evidence of the incredible energy of the quarrymen. They honeycombed these crags with galleries and constructed short railways which, from a distance, appear to defy all the laws of engineering. The fan-shaped screes of slate tinkle incessantly through the remorseless process of erosion in wind and frost. In the late 1950s, five galleries were in use, and the men who worked in them used pneumatic drills. A hundred tons of dressed slate left Honister every month. Richard Brownrigg, the fourth generation of his family to quarry slate, told me of his great-great-grandfather who worked at the top of Yew Crags, dressed the slate on the spot and then packed it on a sled, which he directed down the awesome scree to the road. He had then to carry the sled back again. Some quarrymen lived in shacks on the felltop. A shack on Yew Crags was so exposed that one day the wind blew water from the streams back up the slopes and hurled it against the windows. Looking out at first light, the quarrymen thought it was raining heavily and there would be no chance of work. They stayed indoors all day!

I heard of the frightening occasion when "the wind was in the crack". Such a wind came from the south-west and on a certain precise course was split by the fells. One stream of air went round by Buttermere and was deflected on to Honister Crag by Robinson; the other current travelled by way of Grey Knotts. The two streams met noisily on the face of Honister Crag. A man died when he was tossed over the side by the boisterous wind. It also lifted a wagon containing 30 cwt of slate from its tracks high above the valley.

Lakeland's woodland industries were many and varied. Forty years ago I went looking for details of the old bobbin mill at Skelwith Bridge. I was referred to Mr. Johnstone, who sent me to Mrs. Gaskell, who recommended Harry Wilson as a source of reliable information. Said Harry: "Aye, I can tell ye something about that, but it's a gey lang time sin bobbins were made at Skelwith. Jackson Coward owned the mill. Will Carradice and Tommy Satterthwaite worked there". Harry and I chatted in the yard of his farm. Rhode Island Reds clucked their way to the food scraps. Nimble cats and kittens, spotlessly clean, picked their way daintily over the muddy stones. The story of industrial enterprise that unfolded was, as ever, most fascinating. Harry Taylor "had the lads to feed and accommodate at Mill House. He was allowed so much a week for each lad; it wasn't much, and the lads didn't get so much either". The millowner also kept a draper's and grocer's shop. "All the mill hands had to buy their stuff from him ... He owned a public house and farmed in a small way as well!" As for the bobbins, they were packed into bags or hampers and transported by horse and cart to Windermere railway station. "Jackson Coward brought out a patent for bobbins with cardboard ends instead of wood; it was a good thing. The bobbins were lighter and they didn't break the cotton as often when it was being wound. But some foreign firm got hold of the idea and improved on it. Jackson lost his money".

The restored Stott Park Bobbin Mill, near Finsthwaite, is now a showplace. Woodland was clear-felled every 15 years or so and the wood – birch, ash, alder, sycamore – transported to the mill to be made into bobbins for the textile industry. When I called at Stott Park in 1968, the firm was a going concern. Nine men produced up to 300 gross of bobbins a week. The partners in this enterprise were John Ivison and J.R.M. Coward, the son of John Coward and grandson of William, who founded the firm when he came to Stott Park in 1875. John Ivison grew up at Graythwaite. He saw the time-honoured activities of the coppice woods, being particularly interested in the charcoal-burners who made themselves cabins and lived in them in summer. "Those men looked as black as coal".

When I visited Stott Park, bobbin manufacture had not become a fully automatic process.

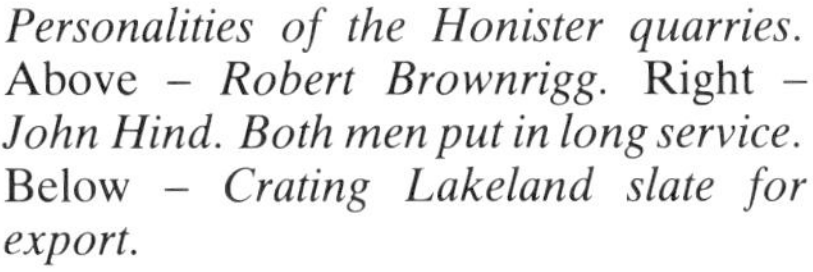

Personalities of the Honister quarries. Above – *Robert Brownrigg*. Right – *John Hind*. Both men put in long service. Below – *Crating Lakeland slate for export*.

Hands grasped levers which brought the wood into contact with cutting edges. Knowing the right kind of pressure to apply was a skill acquired slowly over the years. Originally, the power had come from a wide breast wheel, which served the mill until 1880. Then a steam boiler and turbine were installed. They still existed – in retirement. Since 1941, electricity from the grid had activated the machines. Coppice wood was brought in from a radius of 15 miles. In the 1960s, bobbins were being sent to Manchester, Wakefield, Heckmondwike, Coventry, Nuneaten and London. Shavings were sold to farmers for bedding down their stock. Many a load of unsuitable pieces of wood was collected by local families for burning in the home. I sometimes filled the boot of my car with this cheap fuel.

Alice Black, who lived into her "nineties", was the daughter of a Sawrey man who made his living as a charcoal-burner, being apprenticed to the craft at the age of eight. He worked until he was 65. "We only saw him on a Sunday. He'd set off for work at 4 a.m. and on a summer's night it was often 10 p.m. when he returned. Sometimes he walked from Sawrey to Langdale and back, a round trip of about 28 miles. He earned 18s a week, and there was a family to keep on that!" Mr. Black's charcoal was sent mainly to the tanners of Dunfermline. Some of the charcoal-burners put boxes of clay pipes in the "pits". When the wood had been burnt to charcoal, and the charcoal had been removed, they collected the pipes, which now were quite black. "They were sold as 'seasoned' pipes and brought extra money".

At Spark Bridge, beside the river Crake, lived Jack Allonby, who had personal recollections of charcoal-burning. His family had been engaged in "coaling" for generations. Jack remembered when coppice woods were more valuable to a landowner than agricultural land. The timber regenerated so quickly that some woods might be felled again in 12 years (where the dominant species was hazel) or in about 15 years (in woods consisting mainly of oak). Jack was adept at making a "coaler's cabin" – he did so at the Hay Bridge nature reserve – and he demonstrated that all the materials were handy – stone for the low circular wall; wood for the timbering, which resembled the spars of a wigwam, and "real old fellside sods" to deflect the wind and the rain. A cabin must be kept "aired" and the fire that warmed the men also kept at bay the fungi that would otherwise attack the wood. The hearth was substantial, a sheet of metal deflecting the flames and heat from the roof itself. "A cabin could be a smoky place and building a chimney was a very particular job", Jack observed. "If you didn't get it right, the fire would smoke badly. A draught from the door made the fire roar".

Men were paid an agreed rate per dozen bags of charcoal delivered to Backbarrow. "There were fixed prices for coaling and carting … Father worked on his own. He bought his standing coppice at a fixed rate, usually so much an acre. In 1907, he felled some woodland and made 15 tons of charcoal. That was when a chap was paid by the ton. It was an idea brought in by a new manager at Backbarrow. For those 15 tons, father collected £10 a ton". Winter was a time for felling trees, the season for "winter wood" ending on April 5. After that, oak was cut for the bark, which had to be acquired when the sap was running. Peeling off the bark was an occupation from May to the end of July. The bark was tied up and stored. It had then to be chopped up into lengths for the tanner. In November, the men began to fell the next crop of trees. Charcoal was burnt in "pits", from which any new growth was removed in advance of the new burning season. The hurdles used to control the flow of air to the heap of wood were re-backed with bracken.

Wood to be rendered into charcoal was stacked in a way governed by long tradition, the heap being covered with fine soil (it had to pass through a half-inch riddle). The burning operation was never left unattended. It must not be allowed to burst into flames. Men took it in turns to

STOT PARK MILL, near Finsthwaite, splendidly restored, is visited by many thousands of people each holiday season. To go there in the old days was a fascinating experience, with several men reducing coppice wood to bobbins for industry. Timber fresh from the woods was sawn and "roughed" down to a size just larger than the finished bobbin. It was then quickly dried using a kiln before being finished off.

Bobbin manufacture at Stott Park had not, in the days I recall, become a fully automatic process. Much still depended on the skilful co-ordination of hand and eye. It was a loyal workforce. James Graham, the foreman, was with the firm for 45 years. An advantage of a small concern like this was that it was highly adaptable and could undertake fairly small orders which the largest concerns would not tackle.

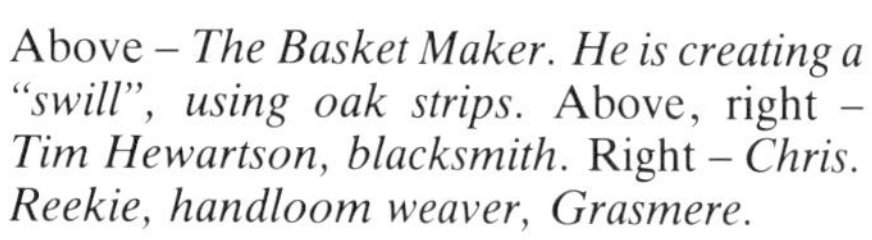

Above – *The Basket Maker. He is creating a "swill", using oak strips.* Above, right – *Tim Hewartson, blacksmith.* Right – *Chris. Reekie, handloom weaver, Grasmere.*

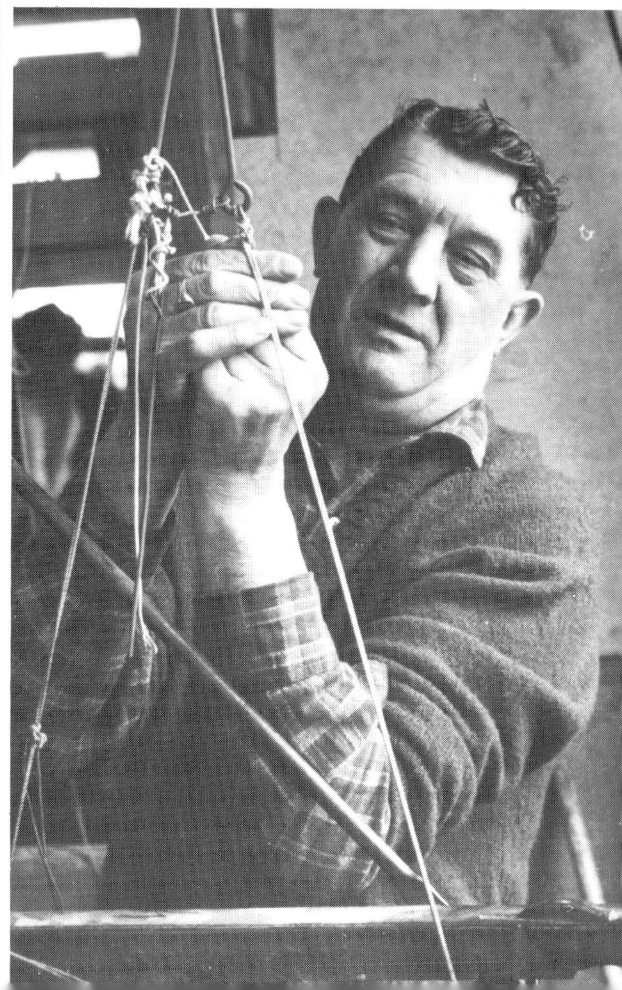

tend it and an off-duty man slept in his clothes. Those clothes were coarse and durable – fustian and flannel. The "coaler" preferred good shoes to boots. Jack Allonby used to say: "You could tell a charcoal-burner by his dark complexion. His eyes looked watery; he was always among smoke".

I asked Jack about the food which the "coalers" took to the woods. He said it was mainly ham and bacon. "Father kept two pigs especially for coaling time. He reckoned on catching a few rabbits. Mother made him some bread, which he kept in a large tin. That bread would keep pretty fresh for up to a week – and in the tin it couldn't be nibbled by mice!" Rodents were attracted by the warmth of the cabin. Adders (or vipers) could be a nuisance. Jack Allonby's great grandmother caught three or four adders. She had left a pan containing a little milk outside the house. When she collected the pan, she found the adders inside, drinking the milk. "Grandmother simply put the lid on the pan and placed it on the fire!" "Coalers" found solace in the chewing of tobacco. Some smoked black twist. "They had some musical instruments for entertaining – fiddle, concertina, mouth organ, Jew's harp". Theirs was a healthy occupation. "Father got a bit of rheumatism, but not too badly. He was round-shouldered, though. We put this down to the fact he was always carrying heavy swills (baskets)".

Jonty Wilson continued to work at the smithy in Fairbank, Kirkby Lonsdale, when he was well into his 80s. He could usually find time for a "crack" about the old days. Jonty began work as a blacksmith at the age of 14. He was an indentured apprentice at the smithy on Underley estate; being paid 2s.6d a week and living at home. His boss was Ted Read, a hulking but genial blacksmith who weighed about 16½ stone. This was an advantage in winter, when he played Rugby for Kendal. "He was a good smith, in spite of his erratic temper. It didn't take him so long to belt a lad if he wasn't doing his job properly!"

Underley, in the days of Lord Henry Bentinck, was a vast place, offering employment for 177 people. There were 16 in the stables, 32 gardeners, 34 foresters, 14 gamekeepers, plus painters, masons, joiners, blacksmiths and a small army of workers in the hall. The stables held 82 horses, 17 of which were hunters. Four Russian stallions were kept simply for drawing the carriage used by the family and friends during the London Season. "We had brougham horses, hacks and three post horses that did nothing else but operate a sort of shuttle service between Underley Hall and the town, collecting such things as mail. "An apprentice smith watched the master, operated the bellows and did any necessary "striking". He worked 12 hours a day, commencing at 6 a.m. "I had one and a-half miles to walk to work, and I left home in the morning at 5.15 a.m. We had to work until 1 p.m. on Saturday".

By mid-century, the Lakeland blacksmith's survival depended on his ability to diversify, to be a jack of a score of trades. From being a painstaking shoer of horses and sharpener of plough irons, he became a goggled welder, a maker of tubular gates and repairer of farm machinery. Few of the old-type smiths remain. For the Fletchers of Levens, the busiest time of the year was November, when the stag fair was held at Kendal. A "stag" is a young, unbroken horse, such as was rounded up on the fells. Trying to get a shoe on to such an animal was "blood for money".

THE NEW FAIR, a June event, was held in the town of Appleby. It then took its chance along the sides of a hedge-bordered road to Long Marton, while the horses grazed Fair Hill. An owner who turned out a horse on the hill paid for the privilege and saw his animal stamped with a letter "p" on its rump to indicate that payment had been made. A section of the road is now blocked off by the police to enable the bargaining to take place without the intrusion of other traffic.

Here I have seen horse boxes, various carts, a blacksmith using bottled gas, virtually every known breed of horse and pony, a goat, terriers, lurchers, dark-haired men – and hundreds of gawpers. One or two good-natured members of the Cumbria Police keep their eyes on every aspect.

A horse trots by, its rider having dispensed with the services of a saddle. He leans backwards, stares fixedly ahead, ready to apply the equestrian equivalent of an "emergency stop" if needed. He shouts at a pitch that could rival the klaxon on a diesel train. A deal is done after some smacking of the hands, leading to the clasp that seals a bargain. This is as good to a traveller as the signing of a legal document. Nobody asks for a receipt. Another man steps in, offering the new owner more than he paid. Within 10 minutes the price has climbed and the now perspiring horse has changed hands three or four times.

At Appleby Fair is a blend of half forgotten horsey smells. Strident voices – oy, oy, oy – are heard above the pounding hooves of animals being displayed before potential buyers. Our picture of some 30 years ago shows a horse and cart bringing friends of the owner back from town.

TRAVELLERS ALL

LONG BEFORE the "travellers" attending Appleby New Fair were confined to Gallows Hill, and before a brave new by-pass gave the whole area a futuristic appearance, I enjoyed the more informal atmosphere. The encampment seemed to stretch for miles along the side of the old road. In 1970, the driest and sunniest New Fair time anyone could remember, James Whitehead introduced me to Silvester Gordon Boswell, a senior traveller, who considered the New Fair was the country's greatest assembly of the gipsy and travelling folk.

He recalled visiting Appleby with his father just before the 1914-18 war; another time, he had visited Appleby with a cart drawn by an old spotted mare, an animal that cost him £8. He also had an Iceland pony, valued at £25. He returned home, after a week of trading, with 11 old ponies and £25. The ponies had been sold to fruit hawkers and "scrapping boys" in Leeds. Now there were few horse-drawn vans on the roads. Mr. Boswell remembered when horses were displayed in Boroughgate at Appleby. Then the Tin Lizzies (Model T Fords) appeared, spluttering and popping, scaring the unbroken colts. The Fair was moved to a less busy area, beyond the railway bridge.

Visiting Appleby in that hot June of 19 years ago, I enjoyed a non-stop variety that was quite free – the ritual of horses being washed through immersion in the river. The animals were urged into the deepest pools by lads riding without the formality of saddles. Travelling folk like colour. Most of the horses I saw were two-tone. A soaking in the river made them look and feel good. Wispy, sun-tanned boys drove horses many times their weight and strength into the deep water until the animals' backs were awash. Then the horses were directed to the bank, where they dried off in the sunshine.

The Fair had attracted about 3,000 travellers, who swarmed into the streets of the town. Some had horses, which were being ridden bareback; others were in horse-drawn carts that were painted in primary colours and screamed to be noticed. (The decorations were mainly horses' heads, in a strong, realistic style). The packed inns reminded one veteran of the days when there were slats on the floor of a hostelry or drinkers would have been paddling in ale. Men sprawled on the grass verges in Boroughgate; they quaffed ale from glasses. Their faces were tanned almost the colour of the drink.

Men tended to loaf about, or to gather in excited little groups for bargaining. The women had the purposeful air of dedicated shoppers, intent on buying the best. "We don't waste anything; neither do we stint ourselves, especially over food", Silvester told me. "We believe that well-fed people don't bother the doctor so much". So the women bought best steak and the firmest onions; they went to clothes shops for frilly frocks and ribbons with which to deck out their small daughters until they looked like fairies. Travelling folk dote on their children.

Gallows Hill is domed, of about 32 acres. In 1970, there was more grass than ever, but the ground was dry and receptive to heavy vehicles. As I walked about the Hill, eavesdropping, I heard a hundred questions directed from one group of travellers to another. "Where have you been?" "How's so-and-so going on?" Someone had died. "What has happened to his children?" There had been several marriages and deaths since the last Fair. The travellers wanted to know all about the circumstances. "We're really one big family", said Silvester Boswell. The travelling folk were well disposed towards me, a stranger. No one objected to being photographed. There was a pride in their vans that encouraged them to show them off. Crown Derby was displayed. It is prized for its colour. "We are little Egyptians; we don't like white, and Crown Derby is pretty, colourful and decorative for the home … We once bought it as an investment. I have some which belonged to my mother; I don't use it now".

It was interesting to hear from Silvester about courtship, which in the old days might lead to marriage at the next re-union – at Brough Hill Fair, in the autumn. Parents did not like their girls to be sly about courting, and so opportunities for meeting boys had to be taken surreptitiously. Secret elopements were once fairly common, but by 1970 marriages tended to be social occasions, like those in ordinary society. Many marriages were solemnised quietly at Registry Offices, such as in Penrith. A young lad would fix his eye on the girl he would like to marry. Year after year, through meetings at the fairs, the friendship would develop. At Appleby, in June, there was little darkness for courtship, but the Brough Hill Fair took place at a time of rapidly shortening days. When it was dark, large stick fires would be lighted, melodions were played, and couples might drift off from the crowds.

Appearances are deceptive. In 1970, I wandered about in an atmosphere of affability. On the day after my visit, Gallows Hill erupted in violence as a quarrel between families was resolved …

The Horse Days are well remembered in all parts of Lakeland. The road up Newlands to Littletown was built in the days when the horse was master of the road. A local farmer recalled for me its state when it was unmetalled, covered with broken stone, with "a bit of earth thrown on to bind it up". The fact that the roads of the valley tend to be all "hills and hollows" did not upset the local roadman, John Tracey, who said: "If roads were all level, people would just drive on. They'd think nothing about the scenery!"

Before motor buses and cars were common, Tebay railway station was busy on Saturdays when the market trains ran to Kendal. Farmers' wives with dressed fowls and baskets of butter and eggs paid the shilling fare and were able to spend the afternoon in town, returning at about 4 p.m. Tebay station handled farm stock. When Brough Hill horse fair and Kendal horse fair were held, the farmers rounded up the fell ponies and despatched them by rail.

John Hind, of Rosthwaite, was a source of rich and varied information about Borrowdale. John could remember when the highway was barely eight feet wide. If two horse-drawn vehicles met, it was sometimes necessary for one to be led into a field to allow the other to pass. The road from Keswick to Lodore took on its present shape shortly before the 1914-18 war. The higher stretches received attention in the late 1920s. The four-in-hands from Keswick were still undertaking the famous Borrowdale round, crossing by Honister to Buttermere and returning to Keswick by Newlands. Horse coaches were operated up to the outbreak of the 1939-45 war.

The memory of prancing horses and liveried coaches remained clear in the mind of John Hind. Up to 16 outfits would leave Keswick on days in high summer. The folk of Borrowdale, knowing that they were due out of town at 10 a.m., kept off the road until they had passed. The horses were watered, and the passengers refreshed, at Rosthwaite. Passengers dismounted for the ascent of Honister Pass. Some people were so over-awed by the steepness of the road they refused to re-enter the coaches for the descent to Buttermere!

Mr. Hind and other local lads could earn up to five shillings on a Saturday by meeting coaches at the top of the pass and attending to the "slippers" on which the wheels rested during

Above – *Fell-top Cafe, on the Shap road, consisting of two buses attached back to back.* Right – *Inside the Cafe.* Below – *The Post-bus begins its return journey from Martindale to Penrith.*

the descent. These wedge-shaped objects, attached to the coach by chain, were slipped under wheels as appropriate and acted as additional brakes. They also ploughed up the unmetalled road, to the annoyance of the road authority. A boy new to the task of "slippering" winced if he picked up a slipper too soon. After slithering down the hill, it had become excessively hot!

Within living memory, road traffic through the Lune Gorge was negligible but the rail services were frequent – and the trains stopped at Tebay. Two branch lines fed the Lancaster-Carlisle railway, one from Clapham to Lowgill and another coming in from the north-east via Stainmore and Kirkby Stephen. Tebay had work for several hundred railwaymen, some of whom manned the locomotives that gave the big trains a push up the bank to Shap. It was taken for granted that when a working-class lad left school, he would try for a job on the railway. There was little else to do. Today, two lines cross an expanse of grass and gravel where once stood an imposing station, closed in 1968. The M6 arrived to absorb much of the local labour. I have chatted with men who remembered when Tebay saw a considerable amount of coke traffic emanating from county Durham. Five coke trains a day ran to industrialised Furness. During the 1914-18 war, Admiralty coal from Swansea and the Midlands was seen on its northward passage through Tebay to Rosyth and the top of Scotland. At Tebay, someone was moving about somewhere in the area throughout the 24 hours. At night, the station had its own gas-house to provide illumination. Even Tebay church was connected to the gas supply.

The most romantic railway journey was that to Coniston. In sunny weather there was an alpine quality about the views from the coach windows. At Bassenthwaite Lake railway station, an evening task was lighting the lamps. The glow came not from electricity, nor even paraffin. The material used was carbide. The "gas house" stood at a respectable distance from the platforms in case of mishap. "It's a bit antiquated, but we get good lights", the stationmaster told me in 1960. "We have got electricity in the station house".

John Tyson, of Threlkeld, served on the Penrith-Keswick stretch of railway. "It was a rather expensive piece of line to build", he said. "The line crosses the river seven times between Threlkeld and Keswick". Mr. Tyson worked on this scenic railway for almost 45 years. When he retired in 1964, he was just short of completing the spell necessary to obtain a gold watch from British Railways and shortly afterwards the period of qualification was brought down to 40 years. The line was closed on March 4, 1972. Then Threlkeld station looked forlorn, with some shattered panes and the main windows boarded up to discourage further vandalism.

"Ratty", as the Ravenglass and Eskdale Railway is affectionately called, was built primarily to serve industry, being opened in 1875 – a time of prosperity in the iron and steel industry – to carry deposits of haematite from around Boot village and Ghyll Foss to the main line of the Furness Railway at Ravenglass. Two years later, the price of iron having begun to fall, the Whitehaven mining company that promoted the railway venture failed. "Ratty" passed into the hands of a receiver, but managed to keep going through catering for tourists. Only four passenger coaches were maintained, but ore wagons were tidied up to provide extra accommodation at rush times.

When the two locomotives were worn out and the track was considered unsafe, the project closed once again, but was saved a second time. W.J. Basset-Lowke, a model-maker, bought the railway, converted the gauge from the old three feet to the present 15 inches – a task completed by 1917 – and used the track for testing his fine engines. "Ratty" now carried all the Mails for Eskdale, plus goods to and from the farms and villages of the dale. The Brocklebank family, who owned the line, were somewhat better known for their Cunard interests in

Above – *Coniston railway station, in the twilight of its life.* Below – *The staff at Arnside, where the station lies near the famous viaduct over the Kent.*

Liverpool! By the 1950s, "Ratty" was in trouble again but, offered for sale in 1960, it was bought by a preservation society under whose auspices it thrives. It is not a toy but a proud little railway which is a delight to tourists and a boon to dwellers in Eskdale.

When John Kirkpatrick was a boy attending school at Shap, in the closing years of last century, he often journeyed to the top of Shap Fell, some five miles away, to watch motor cars trying to reach the top. Not many succeeded. John told me that he left school to become a blacksmith, little realising that the mechanical marvels he had become excited over while at school would eventually bring about the decline of his chosen trade. Edwin Quirk, who had a garage in Keswick for 50 years, remembered the days of Spartan motoring. His family owned the first two-cylinder Wolseley ever made – and the invoice was initialled by the works manager, Herbert Austin. That car, which arrived from the Birmingham works of The Wolseley Sheep Shearing Machine Company in 1900, was fitted with wooden wheels and pneumatic tyres. The invoice totalled £309.16s.4d. The vehicle's speed depended on the size of the front sprocket on the chain drive. A small sprocket was used for a hilly run, but when it was fitted with a large sprocket this car could touch 35 miles an hour on a flat road. One handicap was the official speed limit of 12 miles an hour. No reliable way of judging the speed existed, and the magistrates tended to back up the constables. Those on the Bench owned some of the horses that were being startled by the internal combustion engines. Mr. Quirk, who drove the Wolseley car in 1901, had to brake the vehicle and cut off the engine as a particularly nervous horse was led by.

The Quirk family were living at Workington when they took delivery of the early motor car. Edwin told me that petrol was ordered from Carless, Capel and Leonard, an English firm responsible for bringing the word "petrol" into use. It was originally their trade mark. A case containing four two-gallon tins would arrive at Workington. Women passengers wore two veils – one to intercept any particles thrown up from the road and the other, which was stronger, to secure their large hats. Paraffin lamps blew out in gusty weather and were re-kindled by the motorist under the cover of a cloth, until a firm called R. Bell and Co. devised "Wind Vestas", which burnt fiercely and for quite long periods. These were used by every motorist until electric lighting was introduced. When the Quirks bought a 12-seater charabanc in 1905, it was the first vehicle of its kind to be seen in West Cumberland. Edwin had it with him when he moved to Keswick in 1908.

The first car to rattle down St. John's Vale was owned by Mr. Arthur Hooper, who lived at Beckthornes. It was a steam car, christened "Lily White". Beckthornes was then occupied by the Chaplin family, who in 1910 purchased a K-R-I-T of 20 h.p. Horses shied when the car approached them. Oil lamps were fitted and one dark night it took three hours to travel from Grasmere to Keswick. "As the car passed Thirlmere", I was told by E.S. Chaplin, "my brother stood on the running board and held an acetylene cycle lamp so that its rays touched the boundary wall and I could be sure I was still on the road".

Tom Routledge, of Ambleside, bought a Model T Ford in 1926. The vehicle had belonged to Mrs. Warburton, of Cragg Woods, and it led an adventurous life, including a journey over Honister Pass during which the driver had to ensure there was sufficient petrol in the tank to allow for the gradient, the petrol system being gravity-fed. Mr. Routledge sold the car to a bookmaker at Cockermouth and bought the first of a series of Austins. He worked for the Houghs of White Craggs and the Hedleys of Briery Close and recalled trips with visitors to Lowther Park when the Japanese and Alpine Gardens were open (admission, 1s each). In 1928,

DUNMAIL RAISE – WHEN THE CARS CAME ONE AT A TIME!

he began trips into Mardale, following the old road to the *Dun Bull,* where the Shepherds' Meets were held.

In the 1920s, oil was being refined at Barrow-in-Furness. Mr. W. Troughton of Bowness started work in the employ of the Anglo-American Oil Company, now widely known as Esso. He was a "boy" working on the lorries and eventually he became a driver. "For the first five years, I transported petrol in two-gallon cans and paraffin in a large tank. The paraffin was measured out into five-gallon containers for local customers". When I knew Mr. Troughton, he was operating a garage near Bowness. I heard that petrol had been supplied in cans costing 5p a gallon. When a tank with a capacity of 1,000 gallons was installed at the Troughtons' garage, they had to make their own dipstick. "This we did by pouring in 10 gallons at a time, letting the petrol settle, then lifting out the stick and putting on a fresh notch. Ours was the third bulk tank for petrol in this district".

A number of petrol pumps of distinctly ancient appearance stood outside Bridge End, Ulpha, in the Duddon Valley. Miss V.M. Dawson, in attendance at the pumps, was following a tradition established by her father, James Dawson, in 1927. The old "bowser" pump he then installed was still being used in 1972. It had proved to be more reliable than modern electric pumps. The "bowser" is a hand pump. Seeing Miss Dawson operate it, I recalled a story told to me of the large car that drew up beside a hand-pump. The garage man pumped furiously and then said to the driver: "Would you kindly switch off the engine, sir? You're gaining on me!"

In the case of the Ulpha pump, a gallon was delivered when a rod had been wound to its topmost position, "and then I must wind it back to deliver another gallon … I must be sure to drain the pipe at the end of a delivery, because unlike modern pumps, the measurement starts from the pump itself, not the nozzle. The petrol in the pipe belongs to the customer!" Her assembly of three hand-pumps comprised the only petrol-retailing point in the valley. Father had previously supplied petrol in cans. He must have had a touch of brilliance, for he served his time to shoe-making, yet produced bicycles and converted a Stanley steam car to petrol propulsion with the fitting of a Ford engine. Incidentally, neither Miss Dawson nor her sister owned a car. "We never learnt to drive".

In the 1930s, the roads of Lakeland wandered amiably about the landscape. Today, the major roads must be visible from space, so wide and white are these modern arteries, devised and built in panic to accommodate a steeply-rising number of vehicles. Distance is no object to anyone with a good car. The Birmingham family I met on Helvellyn, at noon, had set off from home, using the M6, that very morning. The old motor route over Shap, with its famous Jungle Cafe and Leyland Clock, carries a little traffic now that the motorway is available. Kendal, once a congested "gateway" to the Lake District, lies between the M6 and its own bypass, which has drawn traffic from the M6 and now pours itself into the heart of Lakeland about Windermere. This road needed attention, of course, but many of us shuddered in 1971 when a dual carriageway of the type one would expect in the suburb of a city appeared to the north of Dunmail Raise. (Old Dunmail must have spun in his grave at this violation of his old haunts).

As long ago as 1934, a time of high unemployment because of industrial recession, the Cumberland County Council proposed that new roads should be made over high level passes. The Honister road was metalled, and strips of tarmac appeared on Wrynose and Hardknott. The A594 (Penrith-Keswick-Cockermouth) was upgraded to a trunk road, the A66, despite protestations by those keen to preserve the countryside. What the planners had in mind was providing an improved road to take traffic from the M6 to industrialised West Cumberland. Why could not such a route be developed to the north of Skiddaw?

Old people recalled when the Shap route was little more than a cart track. Occasionally, a brewer's dray would pass by with a load of wines and spirits for Shap village. Another day, the few farming families gawped as they watched the passage of a circus. "There was no regular and heavy traffic when I was young. Why, 30 years ago (1920s) the volume would not be a quarter of what it is today".

Hand-operated petrol pump, Duddon Valley.

BEATRIX POTTER AT HILL TOP, SAWREY.

WARTIME INTERLUDE

A SMALL WOMAN, grey-haired, but with a face as round and rosy as a cherub, bustled in a Lakeland farmyard, her feet encased in clogs that made a ringing sound on the cobblestones. Men were attending to sheep – Herdwick sheep, of course. The air held the tang of wool grease. The woman watched for a while and then was gone – into a dark, chilly farmhouse. This little lady, who wore a brat or apron made of sacking over her long clothes, was Mrs. William Heelis, wife of a solicitor in Hawkshead. She was also a considerable landowner, with a partiality for little old farms and their stocks of Herdwick sheep.

You will have guessed her better-known name, Beatrix Potter, the author/illustrator of children's books. She who had a stuffy upbringing in a middle-class Victorian household spent her latter days presiding over her Lakeland farms; she lived into the 1940s, when old values and a long-familiar way of life began to crumble. At her home in Near Sawrey she was familiar with an austere way of life, with essential foodstuffs rationed. She heard the Air Raid Warden's whistle, followed by the wavering sound of enemy aircraft intent on bombing the docks at Barrow-in-Furness. The western sky glowed red, as though nature had decreed there would be two sunsets within 24 hours.

Just over the hill from the two Sawreys was Grizedale, its hall requisitioned to hold German prisoners of war. Only one of them escaped and left the country, making his way to North America.

Short Brothers, the aircraft builders, constructed Sunderland flying boats by Windermere and flew them off, many to form part of Coastal Command To see one of these monsters take to the air was awe-inspiring, as I discovered when I went camping near Witherslack with the Boy Scouts and two of us undertook our First Class Journey, with next-to-nothing to eat and only a large square of waterproof material with which to make a shelter. We had dined well, thanks to a farm lad and his ferret. One of the joys of leaving camp was that I escaped the task of skinning rabbits. We had the roads pretty well to ourselves as we strode towards our first objective, the ferry landing just south of Bowness, from which we could sail to a point near Ferry House. The ferry was a coal-fired job, with a slight list on the side where the engine was situated. It was operated jointly by Lancashire and Westmorland county councils. As we crossed Windermere, looking at the cherry-red fire and hearing the hiss of escaping steam, we became aware of a loud droning sound to the north. A Sunderland flying boat, all four engines in lusty action, was taking off. As it passed, it seemed to cast a shadow over half the district.

Forty years later, while conversing with George Pattinson, founder of the Windermere Steamboat Museum, I heard more about Windermere's special contribution to the war effort. Cooper Pattinson, the father of George, was a pioneer of flying boat development in the 1914-18 war, being awarded the first DFC for shooting down a Zeppelin after pursuing it in a F2A flying boat for over nine hours. The Zeppelin was brought down over the Heligoland Bight.

Father was friendly with Francis Short, one of two brothers who manufactured the Sunderland flying boat. He was allowed to board the first craft made at the wartime factory beside Windermere (the site is now occupied by the Lakes School).

Lancaster Parker, the chief test pilot, allowed him to take one set of controls, which he held as the huge craft took to the air. Asked where he would like to go, Mr Pattinson mentioned some family property in Great Langdale. So the flying boat was turned in that direction and, flying low, it traversed the dale, turning over Blea Tarn and then returning over Little Langdale, no doubt to the consternation of local folk and the indigenous sheep. George Pattinson, home on leave from the Royal Navy, watched the flying boat touch down safely. He was familiar with its wartime role, having served on convoy escort duties.

Service airfields were established on the flatlands beside the Solway and the Irish Sea. The high passes of Lakeland were used as training grounds for the drivers of Army vehicles. At Lowther Park, Army tanks, adapted to project powerful beams of light, to confuse the enemy, turned night into day as they were put through their paces (the invention was never seriously used, for by the time it was perfected the great land battles were almost over).

The story of wartime "battles" in Lowther Park were told to readers of *Cumbria* magazine by Peter Connon, who had originally written them up for a publication connected with the Carlisle Great Fair of 1976. His interest stemmed from the stories he heard of flashing lights, intense beams of light and tight security. A local man he contacted had a quick intake of breath and said: "Death rays"! The device was based on the common knowledge that if a bright light falls on the eye, the pupil contracts to shut out the excess light. Conversely, if the light is suddenly extinguished, the pupil dilates in an effort to increase the amount of light falling on it. The theory behind the Lowther experiments was that if a bright light was put through a mechanically driven shutter, set to open and close at a certain frequency, the onlooker would become virtually blind. His eyes would be continually trying to adjust to ever-changing conditions.

For the tests, majestic Lowther saw the construction of Nissen huts. Thousands of tons of wet concrete were poured between its fine avenues of trees. The flashing light device was fitted to tanks. Normal life for the farmers became impossible, most of the field fences and walls being demolished and fields churned up. With no hope of growing fodder crops for the winter, local men had to sell their stock. They were compensated for the loss of animals but none at all for the loss of livelihood. And, as already related, the device was never used as intended. The last tank left Lowther in March, 1945. As Peter Connon wrote: "Lowther Castle was gutted after the war and now stands as a shell. It has the most expensive caravan standings in the world, the sole useful result of £20 million spent on CDL (a code name for Canal Defence Light, alluding to the Suez Canal) at Lowther during the war".

The Royal College of Art had its wartime headquarters in Ambleside. Within moments of entering St. Mary's, at Ambleside, the eye focusses on a painting 26 ft long and about 12 ft high, the work of Gordon Ransom, a student at that College. The picture shows the Ambleside Rushbearing and features 62 almost life-sized figures, including portraits of the vicar and verger of the time. The mural was painted in four months using powder colours with an oil size emulsion.

After I had spoken to members of the Lakeland Writers' Circle, I invited them to contribute some of their more vivid wartime memories to *Cumbria*. The overall impression was of a district whose life was much less affected by wartime conditions than most other parts of the country. D. Howe recalled the day on Windermere station platform when a party of German prisoners

LITERARY LAKELAND
Left – *Norman Nicholson, of Millom, writing while in bed in his attic study. Below – Brackenburn, above Derwentwater, the home for many years of the novelist Hugh Walpole. He created the "Herries" family.*

Above, left – *An old print of Wasdale Head*. Above – *Townend, Troutbeck, the former home of the Browne family, now owned by The National Trust*. Left – *Nab Cottage, overlooking Rydal Water*.

of war – men of high rank – arrived by train and under Army escort and were then put aboard a coach bound for Grizedale. "One man returned to show his wife where he had been imprisoned and was disappointed to find that the Hall had been pulled down, so the memories could not have been too violent or sad". For Marguerite Blake, the most vivid memory was of six German prisoners arriving at the farm by lorry each morning from their camp near Calthwaite. Each carried his mid-day bait, which consisted of a chunk of bread and a piece of cheese. "My mother, a good provider, felt that these men could not do a day's work on the farm with such meagre rations. So each day, she made them either a hot-pot, stew or shepherds' pie, which was always followed by a milk pudding". C.E. Brockbank recalled being taken by her father to the top of the hill near the family home in Kendal so that they might see a red glow in the sky. "He said it was Liverpool burning". A single bomb dropped on a remote farmhouse near Selside. The Technical College in Kendal housed the Heaton Girls' Grammar School from Newcastle.

That Selside farmhouse, Cooper House, was bombed on April 16, 1941. Eleven of its occupants were killed outright. "Those killed were five members of the Wood family, one housemaid, who was a Langdale girl, and five evacuees from London. Two farm men survived, one sustaining several injuries from which he recovered", wrote M.J. Wood. Cooper House was grandmother's home. "I clearly recall seeing, next day, the desolate scene of smoking rubble, where the house had been, and the torn trunks of the monkey puzzle trees which formerly stood tall and majestic in the garden. In contrast, the farm buildings were undamaged and the stock alive and unhurt". Official opinion at the time was that the pilot of the German plane, returning from a bombing raid on the Barrow shipyards, decided to jettison the load. A land mine fell on high ground near Whinfell Beacon.

Mollie Hargreaves's neighbour said she could tell her what happened in wartime. "Nowt to speak of", she said. Mollie, in her contribution to the writers' memories of Lakeland at war, wrote: "Plenty of li'le bombshells were planted on us. Evacuees. I could tell you some tales One boy, nine years old had never seen a pig. Now I do call that deprivation. Not that we minded having them, poor mites. The Big House, they got the interesting Air Force types. We got the kids. Yes, we grew fond of them; you couldn't help yourself ..." A writer signing a contribution A.C.E. was one of a Yorkshire school (requisitioned by the RAF) who was evacuated to a Lakeland hotel. "The boys, ranging from five to 18 years, were a fun-loving gang. War meant nothing to them then, though later it meant a great deal, for Air Training and Army Cadet Units were formed and older boys left to go straight into the Forces".

T. Smithies, serving in the RAF not too far from Lakeland, was able to visit the area on a 24-hour pass. "I used to swear that the immediate area around the Sawreys was not at war with Hitler at all, and that the black-outs were put up only to make things more cosy. No one talked of the war. Eggs, bacon and butter were in unstinted supply every morning, and a gargantuan evening meal was often rounded off with a dream-like Queen's pudding, served with lashings of real cream. No wonder we won the war. The Sawreys were worth fighting for!"

Above – *Chestnut Hill, Bowness, before the chestnut tree was felled.* Below
*– Millom Folk Dance Band gives a special performance outside the
Kirkstone Pass inn.*

ONE OR TWO CHARACTERS

FRANK ROBINSON, of Bowness, lived in a characterful age, before improved transport, the wireless and a movement of populations diluted the old Lakeland way of life. Frank was a person of sharp and original thought. He was unorthodox and unpredictable in his business life but had an abiding love of fair play. His ways of making his goods known to the folk in and around Bowness surprised, sometimes startled, but always entertained them.

His premises on Cragg Brow were a long, low, wooden building erected in late Victorian times. Its windows were packed with fents. In summer you could see caricatures of yourself by glancing in the two large mirrors fastened to a wall outside, one mirror being convex, the other concave. If you were feeling weary and dispirited, the tonic came with the reading of messages on white cards tacked to the woodwork. There was Frank Robinson's business motto: "Poor but honest – nobbut just". He also presented what he claimed to be an old Westmorland toast: "Health of Body, Peace of Mind, A Clean Shirt, and a Guinea".

When I first looked at the shop in the 1950s, I saw his "resolution" expressed as follows: "For the past 43 years I have been diddling the public right and left, and have never been locked up yet. For the next 75 years I intend reversing the process and hope for the best". The author of this verbal magic and the man who kept the tongues of Bowness folk wagging for 40 years was born on June 26, 1863, in a small house beneath the old Wesleyan chapel. He attended the village school and declared that "they used plenty of stick". Afterwards he became apprenticed to the drapery trade. He then left Bowness for London, worked in a drapery store, returned to Kendal, and – as he was to write in local dialect 40 yers later – "Me an't missis felt as t'time was cum ta mek summat fer oursels. Thirty bob a week an warkin' day in day oot, an lile barns ta keep, wasn't a varra promisin' picksher fert future. So tekkin our currige i' baith hans, we exed ta rent t'first middle bit o' t'Fent Shop, as it noo is".

This was on December 17, 1887. His friends soon gave him the nickname of Fenty. He styled himself "The People's Draper". On one side was a fish shop (known as "heads and tails") and on the other a cobbler's shop ("soles and heels"). Fenty's establishment became known as "odds and ends". As the other premises became vacant, he took them over. He was brimful of humour and used to remark that "folk et can't laff et owt that's really funny owt ta see a dockter". Westmorland dialect was his great joy. He was in demand at local "do's", where he recited. He was fond of playing the tin whistle, too, and when people asked him how he did it he would reply: "O ya hev ta do is ta keep liftin' ya fingers up en doon, en blawing et same time".

Frank Robinson was a life-long member of the Bowness Mehtodist Church, and he held many offices A small terrier dog, Peter, went to Chapel with him and walked at his heels when he took up the offertory. Two items of food of which he never grew weary were herb pudding and potted perch. He loved "bass bobbing" (perch fishing). After a day's fishing he would arrive home with between 200 and 300 perch, many of which were potted. The remainder were given away. He died in March, 1945.

John Scoon and his wife kept the shop and post office at Uldale, "back o' Skiddaw", about 1919. Transactions were carried out in the large room in which they lived. John had a beard. His humour was broad and penetrating. His wife had an individualistic approach to life. She sold sweets and cigarettes, as well as groceries, but never really approved of them. She would peer over the counter and, in what could be termed a real schoolmarm tone, rapped: "What deu yeu want?" If it happened to be cigarettes, she would grumble away, saying: "Them dirty cigarette things: Ah divvent knaw what fwoak's thinking' aboot" – yet she sold them! A customer who was in the post office when the telephone range described the terror experienced by Mrs. Scoon. "Oh, deu yeu knaw owt aboot them rowdy things?" she shrieked to the customer. "If yeu divvent, fetch Margy". The customer was able to manipulate the devil's machine and mollify Mrs. Scoon. "I found out that she always went for Margy whenever that THING rang!"

When Bob Fisher, of Staveley, was about 11, his father told him: "It won't be in my time, but you will see the day when there will be carriages going without horses". All Bob could afford when young were some good boots. "I wish I'd as many shillings as times I'd walked to and from Kendal". As a young man, he went to Carlisle to look for a job. He began labouring for a waller. Hard times came, so he set off for home. "I couldn't afford the rail fair, so I walked from Carlisle to Kendal in one day, and had a turnip for my dinner. I sneaked it out of a field by the side of Shap. I could take you to within ten yards of where I ate it". It was about 44 miles from Carlisle. "I left the city just after seven o'clock and I was in Kendal 12 hours later".

In 1951, Mrs. Alice Black – native of Sawrey – showed me a scrap of paper, torn at the creases and frilled with musty brown; two gold rings and an assembly of old photographs – her link with the Lakeland of 1828. The paper was the marriage certificate of her grandparents, Peter Henshaw and Alice Lester. The rings were the wedding rings of her grandmother and one ring was worn to near breaking point. Mrs. Black herself bridged the gap between the leisurely quiet world of the 19th century and the bustling, mechanised world of the immediate post-war period. The last time I met her, she was 92 years old, yet still bright and active. She recalled when Windermere was frozen over. Coaches and horse-drawn sleighs could travel safely on the crust of ice. Coffee was served to those who mustered to skate or attempt to dance and make merry.

I heard of Old Mary Noble, of Hawkshead, who was famed for her cookery, especially "wigs" (long teacakes containing caraway seeds). Dr. Hodgkinson, who lived in a cottage by the shore of Esthwaite Water, made his own pills. James Topping was rarely sober and went about in his bare feet, to the delight of the children, who followed him and, when he settled at the roadside for a sleep, tickled his feet with feathers. He was never in a fit condition to pursue them.

Old Pikky slept rough in stables or other outbuildings and kept a stout stick with which to thump any inquisitive rats. People living nearby would hear the whack of the stick during the night. In the mid-19th century, when there were few toilets in Hawkshead, Mrs. Black's grandmother built three and leased them to local people, who paid their rent half-yearly. Grannie solemnly presented the tenants with large keys, attached to bobbins so that they could not be easily lost.

Wilf Nicholson's smile was capable of lighting up a street. He was most widely known for his Ambleside business – he sold anoraks and boots – but he did much voluntary work. He was a genial secretary of Ambleside Sports. Wilf, who often did the unexpected, went for a week's

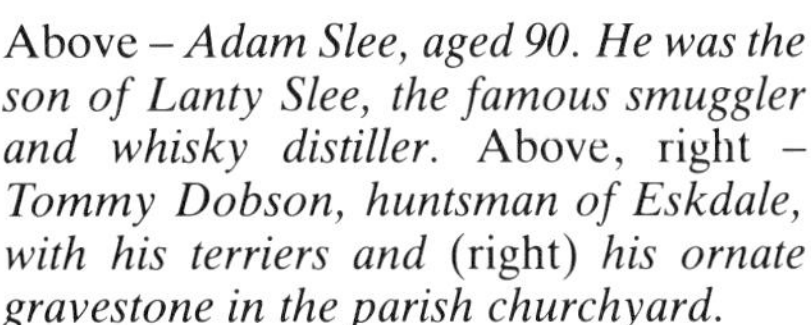

Above – *Adam Slee, aged 90. He was the son of Lanty Slee, the famous smuggler and whisky distiller. Above, right – Tommy Dobson, huntsman of Eskdale, with his terriers and* (right) *his ornate gravestone in the parish churchyard.*

holiday to Troutbeck, three miles from home, where he spent an enjoyable time rabbiting. His father had a sawmill at Winster which relied on water from a dam to provide power for the machinery. Whenever father and his workers were out of the district, Wilf and a friend placed some wire netting across the mill race, let the water rush away and caught dozens of trout, which they sold at 2d each to the villagers. "There was always a big shout when father came back and discovered the mill dam was empty".

Wilf recalled for me one Sports day when an old man approached him and said: "So this is Ambleside Sports. I used to attend 'em when I was a bit of a lad. Where's the finish of the hound trail?" Wilf pointed it out. "Not a bit o' good", said the visitor. "You don't want a downhill finish, young man". Wilf explained that Lakeland has little flat ground. The visitor agreed, looked round at the hills and added: "You got so much land here, you had to pile it up in great heaps!

I once asked Harry Wilson, of Skelwith Bridge, if he had ever been to a cock-fight. "Aye", he replied, heartily. "Seen cock-fighting many a score o' times. Best cock-fight was on Grasmere Island. There's a building there – it's the one that looks like a barn. Folk used to take sheep across from the mainland in a flat-bottomed boat. At certain times of the year when water was low at t'river mouth, they'd drive cows across … Well, it's not surprising folk decided it was a grand place for cock-fighting. The police couldn't interfere. No boats were left for 'em to row across to the island!"

The so-called sport might have gone on longer but the police cautioned the owner of the island, who insisted cock-fighting should cease. Harry took out his clay pipe, rubbed some black twist in his hand, sniffed it in the bowl of the pipe and added: "That blewed that in. But it didn't stop cock-fighting. Men went up to Helvellyn an' Grizedale to meet the lads from Cumberland. A favourite spot was up at Three Shires Stone, between t'passes". Pickets were put out. If anyone came along the cock-fighting would stop and the men disperse. "The latest spot I heard of was up Kentmere. Kit Wilson and Joe Grigg were keen and organised the meetings. Quite a lot o' farmers met for cock-fighting and bets were pretty big. Some gents used to bet as much as £100. Any amount o' fives and tens went on".

"Any sport was man-made", Harry Wilson told me. "We'd throw hats in for wrestling, and on a Sunday afternoon some of the local farmers would come along to watch us. Quoiting was very popular, and to give the police a bit of a job we'd have pitch and toss. You weren't supposed to play it!"

Above – *The bellman of Grasmere Sports*. Below – *Twa lads "tak hod" in Cumberland and Westmorland style wrestling*. Right – *A Lune salmon, caught as part of a hatchery project.*

WIND-SURFERS *(and others) enjoy themselves near Glenridding pier, Ullswater. In this Age of Leisure, every part of Lakeland teems with visitors. It is the culmination of a long process of settlement and exploitation of the landscape that began with the prehistoric folk who hacked out clearings in the forest and continued with the Norse settlers, with the tenants of the monasteries and the yeoman farmers whose austere and thoughtful lives appealed so strongly to Wordsworth. It includes the miners of lead and copper, and the quarrymen who hollowed out some of the fells with shafts and galleries, questing for the best slate.*

Came the visitors – first a trickle of wide-eyed tourists then, with greater publicity and the coming of the railways, a torrent of people who marvelled at the natural beauty of mountain and lake. We now experience a veritable flood of day-trippers and holidaymakers. Lakeland is being modified to accommodate them. Lakeland's beauty has suffered as a consequence.

Roads have been improved, caravan and camping parks established, timeshare schemes and marinas created, new hotel accommodation provided, car parks laid out and provided with litter bins and much else done to house, inform and entertain the tourist. All this development has created jobs – praise be! – but tourism can be a destructive force. Lakeland has lost something of its old character. It has been a lament heard in every generation, for change is inevitable.

CARING FOR LAKELAND

JAMES PORTER, of Eskdale, was proud to be numbered among what he called "the fell folk". He was independent, "beholden to no-one", and as sturdy as a fell pony. James devised the "Felldalesman's coat of arms", which was drawn up neatly by a friend living in Eskdale Green. Above a motto, "The Fells are Mine", was a design incorporating staghorn, a plant of the highest ground. As James remarked to me: "It has a verra strong grip on the grund!" I think of James Porter whenever the path I follow leads me up to the crest of some remote fell, where the clouds sweep low, the ravens utter their gruff calls and a few sheep graze a sparse herbage with all the assurance of animals that are here by the right of 1,000 generations.

Being interested in wildlife, I used to walk alone. The solitary walker sees the fox running from a sunlit bracken patch and the half a dozen red deer that have broken the skyline half a mile away and stare with mild interest at the human intruder as he eats his mid-day snack. Lakeland's fell country was once a succession of solitudes. The first time I had company, my companion was the late and much lamented Dick Hilton, a war casualty. Dick had an artificial leg. We strode up High Street, via Blea Tarn, and I will never forget the slap-thump, slap-thump of his progress.

It was Bob who suggested I might "do" the Wainwrights – all the fells mentioned in the celebrated climbing guides – and I agreed, knowing that Bob would allow time to joke, to chat, and to be quiet in awesome surroundings. We cannot enjoy quietness for long. The Lakeland fells are alive with the sound of fell-walkers. The high hills are being lacerated by many boots. Norman Nicholson wrote about drystone walls that walk; now, as I have already observed, the fells themselves are on the move, being carted away in the form of mud and pebbles on the boots of thousands of visitors. The high-spirited youth who slithers down a scree on Great Gable causes as much erosion in five minutes as nature herself would accomplish through wind, rain, frost and thaw over five years.

Hardwick Rawnsley, a Lakeland clergyman, was one of the trio of eminent Victorians who founded The National Trust in 1895. The others were Octavia Hill and Sir Robert Hunter. Seven years after the foundation, the Trust was able to purchase Brandelhow, west of Derwentwater, this being the first of many acquisitions in Lakeland. Over a quarter of the Lake District is now cared for by the Trust, which nationally has over 1,500,000 members. "Cubby" Acland, agent of the Trust in Lakeland during a period of rapid growth, was rightly proud of the efforts being made to preserve the naturalness of the region. "Cubby" would have been amazed at the situation today.

Almost all the craggy heart of the area, six lakes, a vast acreage of valley woodland, and about 1,500 stone buildings – farms and cottages – are under the Trust's administration. A quite large staff is needed to conserve and enhance what is there. Footpaths are consolidated and thousands of sessile oaks have been planted in old tracts of woodland. The Trust spent over £2,000,000 in Lakeland in 1987. The rate of expenditure is expected to increase with coming years, even taking into account the labour provided by such as Conservation Volunteers and the Manpower Service Commission community programme workers.

The National Trust's major contribution to life in the upper dales comes through its ownership of 80 traditional hill farms and 25,000 Herdwick sheep, which are "on the staff" so to speak, taken over by an incoming tenant who has to leave a flock of similar strength when he moves on, thus preserving the heaf-going instinct of the breed. Representatives of old Lakeland families are given the tenancies of farms; they know about local conditions and are skilled in such as drystone walling. The National Trust's Lakeland Appeal for £2 million by 1991 reached the half way stage by the end of 1988. Much of the money had been donated by ordinary visitors. The money will be used mainly to increase the direct labour force of wardens, builders, woodmen and repair teams. Employment will be found for local people with special skills. The improvement and consolidation of footpaths by the National Trust or the National Park have led to the repair of bridges, the revival of an old technique of "pitching" stones on edge, so that a sort of pavement of large flat-sided stones is created. The Rangers have recently been offering winter training courses for fell-walkers who have just purchased ice axes. The largest single cause of winter mountain accidents is the non-use (or mis-use) of an ice axe.

Forty years ago, Parliamentary approval was given to the establishment of National Parks in England and Wales. They were to be set up to protect the landscape and to provide facilities for public enjoyment – two objects that can easily be at odds with each other in an area like the Lake District. The name "National Park" is unfortunate. The land was not nationalised and, far from being park-like, it usually includes tracts of wild landscape. Almost all of our National Parks lie in the craggy west. Overseas, National Parks are usually uninhabited areas under State ownership and with controlled access. National Parks occupy 9% of England and Wales. It is the opinion of John Toothill, National Park Officer for the Lake District, that to create more would devalue the designation. He observes in his latest Report: "To give special treatment to the best 10% of our landscape (I am adding a bit on for the Broads) leaves an impression of a select elite: to expand that to, say, 20% waters down the product".

The Park Management field staff have put up signs indicating the footpaths and, using Community Programme teams for large projects, have attended to badly eroded fell paths. An example quoted in the latest National Park report is that up Rossett Gill. The dedication of those who set stones on edge to provide a durable, non-skid surface is considerable.

For many years cyclists have followed the green ways and have carried machines for part of the way when travelling across Lakeland against the grain of the countryside. An organisation, the Rough Stuff Fellowship, exists to promote the interests of those who spurn the easy ride. Of special concern in Lakeland today is the increased use of the "mountain bike", an import from the USA. The cyclist is the one who overtakes you as you struggle up a fellside path. (His machine is at least silent, unlike the motor bikes used by a limited number of peak-baggers). The mountain bike's special qualities are its wide-profile tyres. A strengthened frame and extremely low gearing. It can be driven over virtually any sort of land surface. The National Park authority have stated that to ride a mountain bike on an ordinary footpath is an offence.

Among modern conservationists, Geoffrey Berry, who died in 1988, will long be remembered because he left some perceptive books, a library of over 10,000 negatives, featuring every Lakeland hill, dale, lake and tarn, and a reputation for forthright action. For many years he was secretary of the Friends of the Lake District, an organisation founded in 1934. Geoffrey, a Wiltshire man who found a spiritual as well as an actual home in Lakeland,

BOON DAY AT NINEKIRKS, NEAR BROUGHAM.

said: "The Lake District has a sort of intimacy that we must keep". He was an amiable man unless roused by a threat to his adopted landscape. It astonished me that many of those who wielded the greatest influence in the Lakeland of yesterday were men with a gentle nature. I think of Bruce Thompson and "Cubby" Acland, tireless workers for The National Trust.

My last meeting with Geoffrey Berry and his wife Molly was at Brockhole, by the shores of Windermere. He was, as ever, enthusiastic towards the conservation movement. He had retired – to work. Here was one of those Davids who had waged war against Goliaths like Manchester Corporation (over water abstraction from Thirlmere), against British Nuclear Fuels and the Water Authority (with regard to a demand for more water from Wastwater and Ennerdale Water), against the Forestry Commission (with regard to ugly and environmentally damaging afforestation) and against those who would drive great highways through areas of high quality landscape. "Ever since 1966, when I became Secretary to the Friends, I've had a wonderful time", he told Elizabeth Battrick, who contributed a profile of Geoffrey to our Christmas number of *Cumbria* in 1987.

Lakeland has lost much of its old charm. There was a special atmosphere at Gatesgarth Cottage, at the bottom of Honister Pass, when Miss Annie Nelson was here, catering for travellers in the old-time Lakeland way. She was so well-known that the postman delivered a letter addressed to "The Lady at the Tea Cottage (house with table outside), Gatesgarth, Buttermere, Kendal". Every few years, Miss Nelson arranged for the re-painting of the white cross on Fleetwith Pike, a cross commemorating an accident in 1987 when Annie Mercer, on holiday from Rugby, fell and died as she was descending the fell with companions. Miss Nelson recalled when four-in-hand coaches crossed the Pass, the horn being heard as the outfit left Buttermere. Passengers were asked to alight to lessen the load up the steeper stretches of Honister. The road was metalled in 1934. "There was hardly a car came by until it was improved; it was lovely and quiet".

Today, the visitor is supreme. The National Park Visitor Centre at Brockhole was opened 20 years ago, since when about two million visitors have been recorded. The cafe, specialising in home-made fare, has been a particular attraction. The first director, John Nettleton, had Ron Sands as his assistant. It has slowly evolved, with a re-designed lecture theatre, and a splendid permanent display of the Lakeland story, with voices and the calls of wild birds to augment the vivid images. And always at Brockhole there is the joy of walking in the gardens and the grounds that extend to where the short, sharp waves of Windermere break on a rocky shore.

When the Lake District Planning Board advertised for a full-time warden, they were staggered by the response. From a long list of applicants they selected John Wyatt. When I met John, he was still wearing "civvies", though some form of uniform was intended. He told me that he saw his job as that of a benevolent policeman-caretaker. He was out to help the public generally, but he must also enforce the litter acts and local bylaws. He would look after the Board's property in the region. So far his assistance to the public had been concerned with help when cars had broken down; he had also given directions to lost travellers. John told me of being at Cockley Beck, between the high passes of Wrynose and Hardknott, when he saw a man – a very pale-looking man – driving his car backwards from the direction of Hardknott. He had not quite reached the top. "Could you please tell me the way to Fleetwood?" the driver asked.

I would like to think that Lakeland is changeless, but this is something of a myth. Lakeland is changing at a frightful rate. A million visitors a year converge on an area which has a diameter of rather more than 30 miles and they pack valleys that account for a small proportion of the

The spirit of William Wordsworth (above) is everywhere apparent in the Lake District, which he commended so well in prose and verse. Many lines from his poems are well-known, especially those concerning daffodils. He wrote perceptively in a major prose work, his Guide to the district, first published in 1810 as an introduction to a large folio volume of views by the Rev. Joseph Wilkinson and refined and reprinted many times.

Richard Wordsworth, a descendant of the Poet, now lives in a converted farmhouse above Grasmere.

whole. An increasing number find their way on to the fells, where not only is much of the surface vegetation being destroyed but the rocks themselves are being scored and polished by the passage of many feet. Attempts to encourage visitors to tour the outlying areas have only been moderately successful. Everyone wants to see Friar's Crag and Derwentwater, Grasmere and its lake, Bowness and its celebrated bay. In the last year for which figures are available (1987-88), the 11 information centres of the National Park attracted 867,000 visitors and generated an income of £265,000. They are points of convergence for most tourists. At Bowness Bay, a small lecture theatre is well used in summer, as I know from personal experience. The time of a lecture is so arranged that it does not clash with normal meal times at hotel and guest houses. The new Ullswater Centre at Glenridding incorporates a meeting room for Rangers, public toilets with provision for disabled visitors and public telephones. The most memorable display is in a tunnel devised to give visitors something of the atmosphere of the workings at the former Greenside lead mine.

An enterprising project at Thwaite Head, a tract of woodland owned by the Lake District Special Planning Board, has been the production and sale of charcoal. A scheme promoted by the New Woodmanship Trust received National Park support with a grant of £3,000 and a supply of 100 tons of timber. The charcoal burner's traditional activities became a tourist attraction. The intention of the project was to establish whether charcoal is a possible outlet for wood products, thereby making it profitable to bring derelict coppice back into management. An incidental effect was to make the public aware of the importance of the conservation of Lakeland's broadleaved woodlands.

All is not well in the Lakeland farming world. Who, 40 years ago, could have foreseen a Europe with food mountains and farmers being urged to curb their activities so as not to add to the problems. Hill farming is affected because the huge surplus is related to the subsidy policy. The life of a man who farms a slice of a dale and has grazing rights on the relatively poor fells has never been easy. The economics of many of them are now quite precarious.

The best-known Lakeland farms, being owned by The National Trust, will survive intact. Problems resulting from the age and fragility of many buildings and walls will receive attention. Laurence Harwood, the Regional Director, told me: "We must not forget that the purpose of owning farms is to preserve the landscape. Sometimes we have a difficult balance to maintain, between allowing the farmer to do certain things and restraining him from doing other things we do not think appropriate ... The tenants understand our responsibilities ... A special difficulty in the Lake District is that the fell-walking visitor looks almost vertically down at farm buildings".

Elsewhere, at a time when a free rein has been given to market forces, farmers are concerned at threats to the delicate balance of our rural communities. One threat follows the sale of farms. Bill Rawling, of Ennerdale, a prominent member of the Cumberland branch of the Country Landowners' Association, says: "The real worry is that every time a farm goes up for sale it seems to go to somebody who sells off the land and keeps the house. If this trend continues, there will not be a farmhouse left in 20 years' time. And the farmer who buys the land and then wants to put up a house for his family will be caught in a trap. The planning board won't give him permission to build".

Traditional "heafing" arrangements (whereby sheep instinctively keep to the areas of fell on which they wcre reared) are coming under stress. Symptomatic of changes in farming practices and the agricultural economy is talk of the necessity to fence some of the fells. Yet fencing

In the National Park. Above, left – *John Wyatt, shortly after his appointment as the Park's first warden.* Right – *John Nettleton, for many years director of Brockhole, the National Park Centre.* Below – *Brockhole, a most distinctive building.*

would be unsightly and impede the movement of people as well as animals.

Many farmers have already diversified their commercial activities by joining the tourist industry. Their wives provide bed and breakfast for visitors and small caravan parks are in evidence. At Rookin House Farm, just south of Troutbeck, between Keswick and Penrith, Alastair and Ian Hogg took over the 140-acre farm from their father five years ago and turned a run-of-the-mill Lakeland sheep farm into a veritable hive of acitivity, with the addition of riding, trap-driving, and ·clay-pigeon shooting.

Lakeland has a great reputation for hospitality of all kinds. The first association with the Youth Hostel movement was in 1922, when F.W. Parrott, of Kirkby Stephen, visited Germany with a party of Friends (Quakers) and members of the National Adult School Union. In 1930, the National Council of Social Service decided to promote hostels in Britain. Mr. Parrott contacted the organising secretary, Jack Catchpool, and proposed that use might be made of the Friends Meeting House in Kirkby Stephen as a Hostel. This was agreed. The distinction of being the first visitor to the hostel – and thus the first hosteller in Lakeland – went to Charles Bolam, of Gateshead. He reached Kirkby Stephen after walking from Barnard Castle over Stainmore on June 28, 1931.

The possibilities of Newlands Valley, near Keswick, becoming a centre from which visitors might explore the Lake District, and be refreshed by the experience, were seen by the pioneer of CHA, the Rev Arthur Leonard. His idea was to provide cheap holidays for the cotton workers of Lancashire, among whom he laboured. Newlands would be an acceptable alternative to Blackpool. The CHA and Holiday Fellowship guest house in this quiet valley opened many an urban mind to the glory of the fells and dales. An article of about 1913 notes: "The stream serves now as a bathing place for the guests. At half past six or seven o' clock in the morning the call goes round: 'Any more for the beck' and a few sleepy-eyed men and boys wend their way to the bathing pool, while the rest turn over for another 40 winks until the inexorable getting-up bell rouses the whole house".

Denis Bowles was managing the Newlands Youth Guest House of the Holiday Fellowship when I called in 1974. In 1949, it had been felt that the Fellowship should be expanded to take in youngsters. Mr. Bowles was welcoming 4,000 visitors a year.

I began this book with an account of bed and breakfast accommodation at a cottage near Hawkshead 40 years ago. I have not been back to that cottage, but would imagine it has been "improved". Who knows, but there may even be a neon sign in the lounge window? That property had been purchased for a few hundred pounds; now it will be valued at many thousands of pounds. Visitor pressure has created jobs and kept the Lakeland shop tills ringing, but it has also mopped up unused accommodation, seen the conversion of barns into houses and has sent the cost of existing houses soaring, until they are well beyond the range of young Lakeland couples, who must live elsewhere. The newcomers include a high proportion of retired folk. Village schools have closed. Local shops and bus services are fewer than they were. Hotels appear to do well; posh restaurants have proliferated, along with schemes for time-share accommodation and marinas. Now there is talk about providing indoor facilities for visitors – "in case it rains".

Should we encourage as visitors those who wish to be insulated from our Lakeland sights, sounds, scents and weather by breeze block and plate glass? John Toothill, the National Park Officcr, says: "At the end of the day, the National Park should remain a place which people visit because of its natural beauty, not because of some artificial tourist 'attraction'".

Above, left – *Grasmere's celebrated gingerbread shop.* Above, right – *Annie Nelson, of Gatesgarth, who provided meals for visitors.* Below, left – *Will Ritson, of Wasdale Head, as portrayed on a board outside the hotel there.* Below, right – *Potted shrimps from Morecambe Bay.*

My favourite bed and breakfast accommodation was at High Hay Bridge, in an area of the Rusland Valley that Tissie Fooks had designated as a nature reserve to the memory of her husband, Herbert. I would stay overnight after hearing one of Stanley Jeeves's splendid audio-visual shows, which had strong conservational themes and were characterised by "gee whiz" photography and heart-stirring music. Stanley and I slept in beds in the basement and were usually up and about just before dawn so that we might saunter into a Lakeland where the night shift of birds and beasts was ending and the creatures of the day were blinking sleep-mist from their eyes.

We gloried in the dappled woodland and the mossland where, in autumn, each strand of vegetation was draped by a cobweb, beaded with dew. We heard the voice of a roebuck, detected the dank smell of a fox and saw red deer moving as insubstantial as shadows. As the morning developed, buzzards took lift from the thermals and uttered their cat-like mewing calls.

Sometimes, Stanley and I talked, gravely, about the state of the Lake District. Stanley ended one conversation by remarking: "If we're living in an inter-glacial period – and that's what some of these clever scientists are telling us – then there's nothing down here that another Ice Age won't cure!" There is not a single square mile in Lakeland that is truly natural.

Changing Lakeland has been our theme. Change is inevitable. We have dominated the scene for a time-span that is just a blink when set against eternity. Whether Lakeland will shrivel up through the "greenhouse" effect or be refrigerated by another Ice Age is a matter of conjecture. It will not happen overnight. We can go forth and, despite the blemishes, enjoy England's most astonishing tract of country.

Coniston Water, one of the lakes that Arthur Ransome thought of when writing his celebrated books for young people.

BLEA TARN FARM, BETWEEN THE UPPER LANGDALE VALLEYS.

HARVEST FESTIVAL AT THE CHURCH ON CARTMEL FELL